LIFE IS CALLING ...

HOW TO MANIFEST YOUR LIFE PLAN

LIFE IS CALLING ...

HOW TO MANIFEST YOUR LIFE PLAN

STEPHANIE J. KING
(Co-written with the aid of Spirit)

DERWEN PUBLISHING
PEMBROKE · DYFED

This edition published in Great Britain by Derwen Publishing 2011.
Published by Inner Sanctum in 2005 with the title *Just for Today*.
Published by Hay House in 2009.
The author wishes to thank Inner Sanctum and Hay House for the
support of her work.

Derwen Publishing
3 Bengal Villas,
Pembroke, Dyfed
Wales, SA71 4BH

A CIP catalogue for this book is available
from the British Library.

ISBN 978-1-907084-13-3

Production by David Porteous Editions.
www.davidporteous.com

Printed and bound in the UK.

To my family...
Thank you for sharing my life.

To Spirit...
Thank you for sharing your knowledge and guidance.
Thank you for being here with us...

To Paul...
Thank you for helping this book to be born.

(I am I)
You chose to live life in this time frame. You knew what you
would face, the person you'd become and what you felt you
could and wanted to contribute. You knew your talents,
strengths and weaknesses and the path you would travel.
You saw where life would be stuck, what needed to occur
and what you would leave as your mark, as your legacy, as
your own personal offering to life now.

(I am I)

Introduction

In the beginning of time – we could communicate with God, with Earth, with the Universe. We felt warm, secure and loved. Then our ego stepped in. We became torn between our feelings, our emotions, thoughts and mind. We felt abandoned and alone, insecurity, shame, fear, sadness, pain and doubt. We could no longer hear help and guidance being given - we could no longer read the real life signs of life. Today we are still locked within that original negative link, so much so, that for many – life has lost its glow, its purpose; many people are tired, stressed and worn down from their struggle, many are at the point of giving up...

From your first breath to your last, whether you realise it or not, you are embarking on a real, live individual soul journey. You know the thoughts you think, you know your whole life inside out. You know mistakes you've made and maybe are still making, you know the many truths you've witnessed, felt and lived. It is extremely likely that you have lived on Earth before – and if so, that you have helped create today's life as it is. This life and the experience you are having here and now is the most important time of any you've ever had. What has been before - even yesterday, is over, it's finished. What will be the future – who can tell... because each day still to come is yet unwritten.

Yet somewhere down inside you know you are much more – that you're good, that you work hard, that you place others before yourself, that basically you're a good, kind individual... so why should it be that life keeps on falling short, despite the alterations, shifts and changes that we make? What is it that keeps repeatedly going wrong?

Nothing about you is haphazard. You chose your look, your location, your loved one and friends, your home and your surroundings, the food you eat, music preferences, what you laugh and cry at, books you read, vocation, hobbies, work, interests and more besides. You're a living breathing work in continual progression, you are creating and expressing even now. Yet given all of that – how often are you happy? Do you really know what life is all about?

Are you aware you're living a live real time soul journey and that your limited time span here contains targets, purpose, goals? That you have talents, strengths and tasks to accomplish and contribute? That you were born with a pre-chosen life agenda of your own? That you've lived on Earth before, that you create your own reality and that daily life needs and takes instructions straight from you? Do you know you connect to Earth's own creative, thinking mind and that everything about you interacts?

Each passing day is a new chance to create - it's a blank page sitting, waiting to be written. How you use it and what you write is completely your own choice, what you do and how you live is up to you. You are completely individual, free and quite unique, no one else upon the planet is exactly like you. No one knows the life you know or has had the same experience, no one thinks in the same manner – or moves in the same circles… No one else upon Earth's surface can replace you.

Everything you are – connects and integrates, all you've been and ever will be – stems from choices and decisions you have taken. Yes other people interact, but they too are on a journey of their making. They too need to belong, to be loved and understood, they too search for the place they feel they fit. To know exactly who we are we must first know who we're not, and every answer that is needed lies within...

Never before has it been more important for us to wake up to life and reality, a reality we all consciously and subconsciously create. Not only were we born on Earth to live, love and explore – we came to rescue and help loved ones, to grow and make a difference, and to contribute something back to Earth itself.

Life is Calling... will help you manifest your own life plan – and before very long you will know exactly what that is... Labelled a phenomenon and channelled by spirit, this incredible interactive book will take you by the hand a deliver specific, tailored guidance at exactly the time and place you need it most, not only that, but you can share it with your loved ones and your friends.

At the time of your birth you were assigned a spirit guardian, a protector to help you through your life. They not only guard you, but know everything that you do – your faults, your weaknesses and strengths, how others push your buttons, they know everything that's occurring around and to you. They are also very aware of what you wanted to achieve, where you're stuck – and others too, and exactly what you have to do to change that.

We not only connect to each other but we integrate with life, we are directly linked to God Mind here and now. This link has never been broken – we just wrongly thought it was – we directly feed our life force back to Earth. Whenever we want something – it pops up. Whenever we need help – it's always there. All things we think about – compute straight to the planet. Our thoughts, intentions, words and deeds are live instructions.

(I am I). You each connect to Me as I connect to you. I AM the vital living life force that courses through you... You have complete control of yourself and your own life, but everything about it falls back to Me. I cannot intervene or over-ride your own free will. The trick that you must learn is to know, read and understand what's going on. I'll always help and guide you when I can. (I am I)

Life is Calling... is a direct – soul to soul – link to advice for you from your own guardian/angel/guide. A random – open the page – book, you will be led straight to information that will prove relevant from the very first time that you use it. Because you know everything about yourself, your thoughts, situations and events, each time you pick it up Life is Calling... will connect to now, it will be precise in the guidance, words and knowledge being given. It will completely turn around, balance and correct many things you both consciously and subconsciously do. This book has the potential to enhance the rest of your life – for the rest of the time frame that you live here.

(I am I). This book is a direct link back to Me. (I am I).

Manifest your life plan – this is real life – not a rehearsal, and to prove its true your life is calling...

Author's Note

- This work is a three-way link between yourself, your guardian and God.

- Any reference to 'man' in this book is the universal word for humanity, for mankind as a whole. It is not intended to place the male gender over or above the female. They are equal.

- All writing by 'I am I' is channelled directly from God – from the Universal/Earth/Mind energy source. All speak directly with you.

For more information, visit www.channelledbyspirit.com

How to use this book

❖❖❖

LIFE IS CALLING… is an interactive, talking book – written just like cards but in book form. With over 377 cards in total, you could not easily handle such a pack.

It makes a soul to soul link with your own guardian/angel/guide every single time you pick it up for guidance use.

Hold it for a moment between your hands. Immediately you will feel a shift, you'll feel yourself relax. This is because your guardian has stepped forward further into your own space. At the time that you feel ready start to fan through all the pages, just like shuffling, making sure you actually work through every one. Keep on going for as long as you wish. Go with what you feel. There's no need for questions, just let go, relax. You are physically placing your own energy onto all the pages, but so too is your guardian. You're both blending… You'll feel yourself relaxing even more.

At a time that you feel ready – simply stop. Again, go with what you feel. Fan through the pages without looking down or thinking and open up the book at the point you're drawn. Again don't look before hand. If your eyes land on a heading number – just read down. If you land somewhere between numbers – you are mid text, travel up to the beginning of that section, it might even be on the page before. If you are not sure where you landed or you are involuntarily drawn to two – then read them both. Both might be applicable at that time.

Use this book at the very least every morning – that way you'll know for sure that the information being given is for the day ahead. It can be so precise that when you use it in the evening you can wonder whether it's for the day you've had or the one that lays ahead, so to use it in the morning avoids confusion. Use it as many times as you want to in the day – if something happens to you or around you, if a thought pops into your head – whether it's directly linked to you or not, just pick it up and see, because something has passed through your consciousness, there's a good chance that you can help or do or change something about it. You can take this book to work, share it with friends and family, but they too must repeat the procedure to connect to their own guardian.

There is no such thing as energy contamination. The point of shuffling is the point of energy transference and connection. When you get your book back just do the same. Because this is a live, working tool, we suggest you place it in a place you will often see it, like the kitchen, sitting room, coffee table, bathroom etc. Spirit are not fussy where you keep it, just as long as it gets used. It's a working tool to help you, not an ornament to look at... Remember this is a tool to help you in your life – so enjoy it...

Remember that working with Spirit is a two way street. They need us just as much as we need them. On days when you are clear or in an OK place for the moment, they will give you something for someone else who will cross your path, some-one who at that time needs assistance. Just remain aware and pass on the information at the time that it arises, you'll be per-forming a service... Only when we work together, pulling in the same direction, letting go of ego, old patterns, preconception, misinterpretation and outdated emotions, can we fulfil our own souls highest life agenda...

Together we really can combine Heaven and Earth – to bring in peace, understanding and balance. Together we can bring in the light...

1

❖ ❖ ❖

There are many people in this world, each on their own path, living their own life and moving towards their own destiny. This is good. This is how things were meant to be.

Every human being is born individually. Each member of any family is individual. Every person born to the earth is unique.

The life we are given is the sole responsibility of the owner. What we do with our time and the path we choose to tread is up to us entirely.

People may think they are at the beck and call and mercy of others but the opposite is true. We have the ability to choose for ourselves whether we follow or not. This is how it should be.

Just for today, notice the tune that you dance to. Is it one of your own designs, or do you move to the rhythm of another's choice?

2

❖ ❖ ❖

There are always two trains of thought: One positive and one negative. Stay in the positive whenever possible – to keep out of harm's way.

The thoughts we think are not as private – nor as innocent - as we believe they are. Many are left to chatter away uncontrolled, all day and everyday.

Man has the ability to move mountains. There is nothing he is unable to achieve once he sets his mind to it, and this is the key. The thoughts we think have the ability to do all and more than we could ever imagine.

All thoughts produce energy that is either positive or negative in nature. They are in fact forms of energy themselves. They are energy in motion and therefore have a final destination and purpose. Thoughts produce the energy that determines our next course of action. They form the next things we will do or say. They supersede all that man ever does. They set intention.

Just for today, recycle the thoughts that bear no resemblance to your now. You should hold onto nothing that is inappropriate to the moment you are in, the moment you are experiencing. Choose the thoughts that move through your mind with awareness that you are creating your own reality. Empty your mind bin as often as you can to remove the clutter that keeps you clinging too tightly to the past.

3

❖ ❖ ❖

Many people find it easier to worry than to trust. To trust means that you stay in the love at all times with your thoughts. It is by remaining in the love, and only then, that miracles can occur.

Miracles are not just incredible deeds that exist in the Bible. They are common everyday occurrences.

To see them we must be totally in the now, and to stay in the now is to stay in the present with your conscious attention, not in the future or the past.

Miracles also require that we stay in a state of love, not a mushy, air-headed kind of love but in a constant state of truth, balance and love for the world that you live in, the world from which you operate.

A positive frame of mind induces a love state that sees the best side of everything you encounter. It allows the love to flow unchecked through your day.

Like attracts like. Negative energy is fear in action. It produces stress, worry, anxiety, anger and other blockages. Positive energy is open, it is love in action. It allows life to flow with greater ease of its own accord. It keeps your spirit up and your energy high. It allows the seeming impossible to occur. It paves the way for miracles to manifest.

Just for today, notice the unexpected. Notice the little things that seemed to fall into place of their own accord.

4

♦ ♦ ♦

Many men forget that they are human. Man is not an infallible machine.

Yet man is a machine nonetheless. He is a living, breathing, growing and creating genetic bio-chemical mechanism.

It is the duty of man to experience and express the essence of life itself. He is master of all he surveys. He is the creator of his own universe.

Life is never constant except in its state of fluctuation. Life is also not guaranteed. The choices we make are completely up to us. Mistakes happen – so choose and choose again until you are happy with your lot.

Machines are able to go on and on, but the needs of man alter as often as the seasons change themselves. Go with the flow of the life that you choose. Time is short – so aim to choose well.

Just for today, be aware of the quality of your choices and your human factor. Keep your aims realistic and firmly in the now. Keep your feet on the ground and your head clear of illusion.

5

❖ ❖ ❖

Trouble will always come to attack your day. It is up to you to remain above and unaffected by it.

Trouble is part and parcel of life. It comes in many guises and can ruin a perfectly happy day in seconds.

Trouble is not there to make us buckle under its weight; instead can be a means for growth. It is nature's way of clearing the old to make way for the new. It can force us to look at situations that in reality should have been checked long ago.

Trouble is a way to clear the air – just like the thunderstorms of nature. It forcibly removes blockages that otherwise close our way to a better flow of life.

Just as the tide must ebb and flow, so must the currents of life. We can either wallow in our sorrow at the things we encounter, or we can look for the clearest and most effective solution to the problem. The choice is ours.

Just for today, notice the trouble that you encounter. Silently ask that it can be recycled for your highest good. Ask that you can remain as small as possible to enable it to blow over quickly.

6

❖ ❖ ❖

I must learn to stay in a positive frame of mind at all times. Only this can lead to peace of mind and a greater understanding of the situation at hand.

A positive frame of mind is not always easy to obtain and then retain. Only a quiet mind can look positively outward at what needs to be addressed. Stress is today's most common complaint of the mind as we expect it to multitask at every opportunity. Not only this, but we are receptive to the stress vibrations of others as well.

At the first sign of stress within yourself, stop and take some long deep breaths. Bring your mind back to a central, peaceful position. Focus on the task you are performing or must perform next. Address only what needs to be done now. Take one step at a time exactly as it arises and keep yourself centred and calm throughout.

Stress is a symptom. It is a sign that you are being pulled in too many directions at once. You are not a machine.

Just for today, mentally send your thoughts upward and ask for your stress to be removed. Ask that your energy can be as small as a grain of sand until the onslaught is over. Ask that situations around you be recycled and returned in the manner with which you can cope. Ask that you receive both peace of mind and the energy you need to take you comfortably through your day.

The more you recycle your stress and the clamouring of thoughts that it brings, the more you will keep your centre of mind in peace and balance. Only this will give you a positive connection to the moment at hand.

7

❖❖❖

I must remember that it is what I do in this life that counts.

Life is like a symphony in motion. Each person must live the part that is unique to his or her self. The promises we make to ourselves and to others remain null and void, without action behind them to bring them to life.

Actions are the creative manifestation of thoughts we have had. Only physical manifestation can gather life unto itself

Thoughts remain just that – thoughts. Only the things we do and say can play the part they must in the scheme of life.

Only that which we have built and shared can stand up in our favour at the time of our reckoning. Only things we actually do can leave their mark.

Just for today, do all that you know must be done. Put your thoughts into physical manifestation and let your deeds speak up for themselves.

8

Despite the storms that rage around my head, I must remain in the light and the love of God at all times.

During the heat of an argument and at the height of stress it is easy to loose your composure. Just as a pressure cooker lets off steam, we seem to feel better when we scream and shout. But that is not always the answer.

To scream and shout at another is to lose your own inner balance and relinquish your energy advantage. By giving in to the negativity of the moment you add more negative energy to an already volatile situation.

Like attracts like. That is the nature of physics. To become part of the storm is to be based in the fear of the moment. By remaining calm and open we can more easily attain the truest solution.

Just for today, recycle any negativity that surrounds you. Hand it up to God – for your highest good. Ask that your energy field be as small as a grain of sand and for all others around you to be the same. Take some deep breaths until you feel centred and calm enough to continue.

You are now firmly in the light once more.

9

❖❖❖

I must remain small, especially when my mind is clamouring over itself with runaway thoughts.

The body you own is not the total sum of your whole self. You are much more. You are an energy matrix that is capable of life in a bigger sense. The part of you that can laugh, cry, love, feel and remember is the part that is pure energy. This is the real you. This is the part that existed before you were born and will still exist after your body does not. This part of you can never die – it simply returns home.

Your body is the vehicle that allows this matrix (the part of you that is you) to move about and experience life in a physical manner in a physical world. You are neither your arms nor your legs. If you lost any part of your anatomy you would still be you, perhaps encumbered – but still yourself nonetheless.

The essence that is you, your energy body, is actually larger than your physical one. It protrudes beyond the boundary of your visible outer shell. During normal daily life it acts as a real time life scanner. It helps you feel and read situations. It is your guidance and survival mechanism. It is the blueprint of all you have seen and done since your life began. This part of you is unique to you and you alone. It is you.

Just for today, realize that your energy body needs pulling back into your physical one at times of stress, disorder and discomfort. By asking to be small you are doing just that. You are battening down your hatches and allowing exterior conditions to blow past until normality returns. Ask also for your mind to be still and your thoughts to be at peace.

10

❖ ❖ ❖

I must learn to value myself.

How much do you think you are worth?

To those who love us we are priceless. To those nameless faces with which we interact in a normal working day we are probably worth very little. But how much do we value ourselves? How much should we value ourselves?

Each one of us is an integral part of our working family unit. We are the pillars and stabilizing posts. But to the rest of the world we are replaceable. We are little different to the person who came before or will come after once we have gone. We are all the same as one another.

Yet each and every one of us is worth more. Much more. We are irreplaceable in the scheme of life itself. Just look at Leonardo da Vinci, Newton, Einstein, Isambard Kingdom Brunel, Alexander Graham Bell... The list is endless. They were extreme – each of them individual, yet the same in many ways as you and I. They each offered their absolute best within their chosen field – to benefit the many.

Just for today, take a look at yourself. Take a look at the lives you affect and effect. Notice how things would differ were you not around.

In the scheme of things your life is worth more than you think. Use it well.

11

❖❖❖

I am learning to stay focused on the present.

The present is the here and now. This moment you are in. It is neither the past nor the future. It is not even this morning or this night yet to come.

During the course of a busy day we leave much of the present moment to automatic pilot. Our mind wanders freely wherever it chooses and we merely go along with its thoughts.

Just for today, try to keep your mind focused on only the task at hand. Send your thoughts up, for the highest good, and ask that you be given some help to remain focused fully in your present. Each time your mind begins to wander, ask again. Ask that all unnecessary thoughts be recycled and removed. At the end of the day notice how much better you feel and how much more you have achieved with your time.

12

❖❖❖

I must please myself as often as I please others.

Pleasing yourself is not just a question of indulgence. Nor is it disregarding your responsibilities and commitments. It is about balance and being in tune with your inner needs. It is about not ignoring things you must put into action to keep your own life smoothly ticking over.

During the course of our life we try to live as easily and as happily as possible. We help others and put ourselves out. We feel good and of value as we prove that we care. But how often do we give our own self the same consideration? How often do we deprive ourselves of what we enjoy most – the simple things in life?

Just for today, take a few minutes out of your busy schedule to sit still in the sunshine. Sit down and deliberately take time out just for you, as you would happily do for someone else if you were asked.

13
❖❖❖

I am safe and protected in all that I do by the hand and the love of my creator.

The world that we live upon is a living, breathing organism. Thoughts we think are individual to us but they also combine as part of the universal consciousness. Nothing we do or say belongs to us alone. It belongs to the creative force of the planet.

Man lives his life by his own free choice and free will, but he is also an integral part of the all that is. He is part of the planet that he lives upon. He is part of the system that keeps him alive – and always will be.

Man was placed on this earth to experience and to live life to the full. He may do this in any way he wishes. He alone can play his part as conscious mind tries to know the feelings and meanings of all it has created.

Man is the bringer of knowledge and experience back to the creative, as a modem downloads information to each individual computer, so man feeds information to the collective consciousness.

It is up to each man individually to recycle the clutter and darkness from the corners of his mind; and in doing so he will clear the way for truth and clear sight.

Just for today, be aware of the thoughts you think and notice their influence on what you do and say. Only when you are internally balanced and at peace can you be sure you are seeing truth without illusion. When you can answer 'yes' to these things you are seeing through the eyes of the creator and are safe in its protection and love.

14

❖❖❖

I am an inspiration in my own right.

The life we have is ours to use, however we see fit.

No two pathways can ever be the same because they are individually created by our surroundings, our lessons, influences, beliefs and free choices. The life we have lived until now must be happily seen as our own creation. Each day we do all the things we do because we choose to. Hourly we make choices that instigate our reality and build up our life in the way that we think it should be.

The route your life will follow from this day forth is also by your own design. You are your own creative force and the instigator of all you will become.

The books you read and information you subject yourself to will play their part, but at the end of the day they are mainly the thoughts and experiences of others. From time to time buttons inside you might be activated as your interest is captured for a while, but never forget that you are the creator of your own person.

Just for today, own yourself. Notice who you are and what you want, be the best version of the self that you know you can be. Be you.

15
❖❖❖

I must go with the flow of life.

Life goes past in seconds yet the time allotted to each span is but a flicker in the flame of this planet's existence.

The day we are in now is the most important one that we have. It is the link to the rest of our life as it separates our past from our future and gives us the power of creation.

Yet how many of us really notice individual moments themselves? This day and its now is already spent with every appointment and future plan that we make in advance, and the problem is that we do this so well we don't even realize. We place the majority of our time on automatic pilot.

Just for today, take a fresh look at how you spend your time. Separate necessity from automatic. When you get a chance to slip in some spontaneity, then do so. Take advantage of an extra-unexpected opportunity and go with the flow. Life is never rigid and neither should we be.

16
❖❖❖

I can only do my best at all times.

The best we can do – what does that mean? This can vary from person to person, day to day, mood to mood and moment to moment. Our best in conversation might differ when the actual time and event arise. Our best thoughts and intentions do not always materialize into best action.

The best we can do might be limited to money, time or a busy lifestyle or schedule. It may be hampered by mood swings or the opinions or influence of others. The best we think we can do might be less than we actually manage at the given time. Sometimes we surprise ourselves and sometimes we can fall short of expectation. But there is the key. At any given time what do we expect we should do? What do others expect of us? And are those expectations realistic or far too tall to ever be achieved?

Just for today, notice the reality of your achievements. Remove all illusion and be realistic in your goal. Don't overstretch yourself, but don't be stingy either. Your best is the best result you could hope to achieve at the given time the circumstance presents itself.

17

✦✦✦

All of us are interconnected through the Earth we all live upon.

The planet upon which we rely for our sustenance is also reliant upon us. We play a far greater role in the scheme of life than we presently understand.

Each person is an individual in his own right, but each individual connects and interconnects with others through the routine of normal daily life. A house has many rooms but there is no cut-off point to separate the air that flows between its rooms. It all combines to become a part of the house. And so it is also with us. There is no dividing point between the energy that is ours alone and the energy that is part of another person. We intermingle and integrate as energy flows freely at all times. We are all part of the same whole.

Just for today, be aware of the energy of people that come into contact with your energy field. Notice whether they uplift you or pull you down. Notice what you give and take as you communicate and interact with one another, whether they increase your confidence or make you nervous. The force that flows through us all is the same. It stems from the Earth itself. It is our joint connection to the planet and to this life we are living.

18

❖ ❖ ❖

I am aware of those around me that I cannot see. Although I cannot see them, I acknowledge they are there just the same.

This body we have is the vehicle that allows us to experience a physical lifetime. We are energy beings that use our bodies as an outer shell in a physical world. We need them to feel, enjoy and explore within the density of this planet that we live upon.

Man is much more than his physical body. He is a living, breathing, feeling and experiencing biochemical being. The body you have now is only of use in this lifetime. Once this time is spent it will drop away like a chestnut drops from its shell. Man exists before he is born into this body and he will continue on after it has left him. He cannot die because he is instead the part he cannot see, the part that loves and feels and cries and knows. He is his spirit. He cannot die, because he has eternal life. His spirit is his real self.

Man does not walk this earth alone and he does not face his daily grind alone either – even though he believes this to be the case. Those we have loved and lost through time do not disappear and die, they simply go home. They go back to the place we all came from, they move forward in the spirit world and continue living life without the heavy body that they had. They drop in to see us, sit with us just to be with us - and help us as often as, or maybe more often than, they could before. They remain a part of life we cannot see without second sight.

Just for today, become aware of little things that help you throughout your day; notice when information drops into your life at the time you were thinking about it. Notice chance meetings with people you needed to speak to or see, or when something falls into place more easily than hoped. Notice the help you are given and voice a silent thank you from inside.

19

❖❖❖

I must be myself at all times. I must be all that I am despite the circumstances around me.

I must be myself. What does that mean? It can mean different things to everyone, every day, but it does not mean be selfish or arrogant.

To be yourself you must know yourself. You must look at life with nothing more than the moment dictates. You must have no preconception, false impression or cloaks that surround you. You must be an unwritten page from the book of your life.

Circumstances that surround you will try your patience and influence. But only when you are fully in the present can you truthfully weigh up the situation.

Be aware of any decisions you make and of thoughts that filter through your mind to help you. Are you connecting to old or similar events from your memory bank, or perhaps from a position of fear; fear of what will be, or fear from another angle?

Just for today, try to approach each situation with an open view. Try to live this day on its own merits. How can you know the outcome when the experience has not yet been lived?

20

◆◆◆

I must listen to my body when it says it needs a rest.

The human body is very versatile but it is not an unbreakable machine. It needs fuel and maintenance, just as you would maintain your favourite car. It needs food for thought as well as food for energy, but most of all it needs attention and care.

Many confuse attention with over indulgence. There is no need to lavish time and effort on your body for days at a time, but we should listen to the warning signals it sends out. How many of us drink enough water? How many times do we choose junk food over healthier, balanced meals? We go to bed too late and push ourselves too hard.

Today's fast living demands much. We can do it all – but we must take better care to balance the rough with the smooth. When your body has been pushed to the limit allow it some consideration. It is the vehicle that helps you enjoy all that your life dictates. Be aware of the little signs that say you have reached a limit and notice when either another or you ask too much of your body.

You are a work of art. You are unique. You create your life...

Just for today, notice the way you treat yourself. Are you very demanding? Be aware of over stretching your body's resources or of undue laziness. Try to balance your activity with good food and rest. Be as respectful of your own self as you are of other people.

21

◆ ◆ ◆

I must learn to trust my own judgement.

In life we find it far easier to trust in the advice of another than to trust in ourselves. Yet what do others really know about the difficulties and decisions we have to face? They know only the little that we tell them or have allowed them to know. They know only their own experience and the things they have learnt or have heard.

Reality can be somewhat different.

Only you know the life you have lived and the trials you have had to endure. The situation you are in is unique. There is only one of you. Your problems possibly lead you down a different route to those of your friends and colleagues, so your solution will be individual as well.

Trust in your own unique guidance. Trust your instincts. The place you are at now is the exact place you were meant to be, for without it you cannot reach the next step, the next phase of your life. Embrace your problem and look closely at what needs doing to correct it – for good.

Just for today, trust your own judgement. You have far more capability than you realize.

22

❖❖❖

I must learn not to be afraid of the anger of others.

There is nothing positive about anger. There is nothing clever about screaming or shouting, yet we all experience or do it from time to time.

Anger is the place we go when we don't know what next to do, when we feel used, misunderstood or vulnerable, when we have used up all options or feel we have been wronged. Anger is nearly always counterproductive. It attracts nothing but negativity and can fuel an already volatile situation even further. Negative energy produced by anger does not simply leave us after it occurs but bounces from person to person for the whole of the rest of the day. We move it or hold onto it with our behaviour even after the event has long finished.

When you feel anger or see it in another, step back, reassess and look at the situation fully. Don't take their anger on board as your own but remain balanced instead. Look behind the scene to find the cause of the outburst. Look deeper for the truth and understanding that lie there.

Anger is energy that has become negative through miscommunication, misunderstanding or neglect. It is peace temporarily shattered. You yourself hold the key, you can choose to let it go – to restore balance and unity once more.

Just for today, if you come across someone's anger or feel it welling up inside of yourself – take a moment to stand back and still your soul. Take some long deep breaths and send your thoughts upstairs. Ask that all illusion and negativity be recycled, that peace and balance return and that the situation be cleared up as soon as possible, then move on.

23
❖❖❖

I am loved.

I am loved. Three small words that man needs as much as the air he breathes. Words he searches for to fulfil his entire life.

From the time we are born we learn to respond to feelings that love will induce. We learn how best to behave to receive more and how to give it back to the source from whence it flows.

When we know love in abundance right from the start we have little difficulty in fulfilling its presence through the years that follow, but when we must earn or fight for that love we become insecure. We feel we must constantly prove our worth for the love that we need from each other.

Yet this is a fallacy. We are all worthy of love – despite our flaws. Never before has it ever been otherwise. We have been misled.

Just for today, put aside your doubts and believe in your true self. Realize that all your life you have lived in the search for recognition and approval. Realize that no other person can give you what you already possess. Realize you are made from love in its purest form.

Understand you are a child of this Earth, the son or daughter of the creator and an important part in the structure of all that is; and in so being realize you are the essence of love and life itself.

24

❖❖❖

I must ask for help when I need it.

In this life there are many challenges and many opportunities to stand tall – and to fall down.

When we ride high it is easy to go from strength to strength, both under our own steam and with the help of others, but when we are low we feel bedraggled and lost in a life that seems to not notice our struggle. We seem dogged by misfortune or the errors of circumstance.

Just for today, send your thoughts upstairs, to those who are waiting to help you, not in this world, but in spirit's parallel one. Ask that all negativity and illusion be recycled. Ask that truth and love and light be your guide and that your day be uplifted to a more positive level. Ask that you can remain as small as possible to let any adversity you encounter pass you by.

The help you need is only a thought away but unless you ask for and notice it, that distance may just as well be a light year.

25

❖ ❖ ❖

I must place all things firmly in God's hands before I try to decipher them myself.

Life is a personal journey. It is different for us all. Even for family members that share all the things that they do.

Along the course of life it is natural to meet others who want or need help, so we give it, but how can we know what they need? They too are on their own individual path, a path that merely touches ours in friendship and in love. We can lend our ears and our time but it is wrong to remove their encountered obstacles completely – even though we might want to. It would be wrong to rob them of experiences those obstacles themselves represent. They are life's lessons that will aim to take them forward.

Just for today, link your thoughts to the God mind. Pass these people and their needs up to God, to Source, not because you don't care, but because you most definitely do. Ask that they may receive the guidance and the love right for them at this time, and watch the difference in the way they then move through their situation. If you are still to help, ask that you be shown the best way to help them encounter their solution.

26

◆ ◆ ◆

I must speak my mind at all times, but with love and understanding, not annoyance.

Only two trains of thought exist: fear and love; there is nothing else.

Fear is negative thought. When we are down and stressed-out, angry, anxious or jealous we operate from the negative. We see life from a troubled perspective and add even more to our situation with the troubled thoughts that we think. We are closed and alone in our mood because we unknowingly operate from within a grey area.

Love is the opposite. It is light and uplifting. It can punch through a tricky situation just as easily as we can blink our eye. The love mode is open and none judgmental. It is as carefree and as innocent as a child. When we operate from within it we are balanced and able to understand things better. We view life from all angles because we are open to the help being offered.

Just for today, ask that you may operate from the love. Ask that you can remain balanced and at peace and that all negativity be recycled.

Ask that your guidance be of God.

27

♦♦♦

If I pay attention I can see God's connection in all things.

You are connected to God. All things are connected to God. There is no exception.

The life that gives you life is life itself. It is the body of the planet that man lives upon. Again there can be no exception.

Man is not as alone as he thinks. The life he lives is by his own design and he is responsible for the energies he transmits. His life is his contribution to the whole. His contribution adds to the energy of the planet. It is fed through out his whole life to the whole.

Just for today, be aware of the life that is yours. It is the input you offer to the planet. The life you must weave will leave its mark long after your presence has past. The Earth deserves no less than the very best you can possibly give.

28

❖ ❖ ❖

I must learn that questions are a good thing. They stimulate growth and understanding.

In the beginning there was nothing but the energy that was God. It wanted to know itself and from the questions it had it began to take form. The planet that became its body was formed and the Earth we now live upon was born.

Man today has similar questions. He wants to experience all he can think of, all that he comes across and all that he knows is possible. He similarly wants to experience the impossible and stretch his boundaries to the limit — and more often today, to the extreme.

Children question everything. They build their foundations and boundaries upon the answers they receive. They believe all they are told by peers in their circles, because they are too young to discriminate themselves. They have no means to measure against positive and negative, truth and illusion. They simply accept all things as they experience them to be.

Just for today, look at all you see through the eyes of a child. Examine every situation from an innocent perspective and discover what it is trying to tell you. Unlike a child you have a data bank of experience to draw upon. You already know the differences between right and wrong, and more besides.

29

♦ ♦ ♦

I must please myself.

The planet we live upon knows what must be done for its survival. It is a genetic bio-machine that follows a natural order. Man also has natural order to his life. This is the way it should be.

The balance of life will shift and change as the needs of man ebb and flow. The planet, however, cannot alter what it does. It cannot alter its natural rhythm.

Man has become the creator. He lives and becomes his choices and fears, his intention. He has far surpassed his original limitations. He lives the life he builds and he takes whatever his needs dictate. The Earth has no way to prevent him. It waits for man to wake up.

Just for today, be aware of the content of your day. Notice the demands you make of others and of those you make of yourself. Check your life is moving in the direction you think it is. Become aware of unnecessary things you do. Notice whether you please your needs of living or whether you are wasting them. You have sole responsibility for the offering of your life. Please yourself but be aware of the thread that you weave. It is your legacy.

30

❖ ❖ ❖

I must speak my mind at all times.

We listen, we talk, but do we always say exactly what we mean to say? Do we say what even needs to be said? The answer is that we don't.

Conversation must pass two modes of understanding before it hits the spot. It is reliant on the mood of the speaker as well as the recipient. The meanings we intend our words to convey and how those words actually get interpreted are often miles apart.

Speech is limiting enough before words are put into context but to complicate matters more we voice them in the way we think they will best reach their target. We colour them to fit the situation and the moment instead of remaining open and honest about our feelings and thoughts. Words do not need to be pointed. They are not tools of anger and pain – put simply, are a way of explaining your inner self. Words can help others understand the place you are now and vice-versa. They can highlight where misunderstanding sits and pave the way for balance, harmony and forward movement.

Just for today, ask that you be given the best words to communicate your true self successfully. Let negativity be recycled that you can remain firmly in the truth of the moment you should be experiencing, so you may act accordingly. Say what needs to be said, but only from the angle of truth and love. Your input is more necessary than you know.

31

❖❖❖

I must not try to fathom out the lives and woes of other people. Instead I must send them love and light and the tools to sort things out for themselves.

The journey we live is as individual as we are. The map we are to follow is unchartered, with each traveller as unhindered as his route.

Man is the creator of his life as well as the majority of situations he endures. He is the keeper of his own thoughts, his own dreams and his own being. Nothing is written on the page of his day until he chooses what to write there himself.

Every day of his life, man must live as he sees fit. He should aim to become the best version of the self that he desires to be, but this also means the best at working through his problems and mishaps. The way he chooses to pass these obstacles is also in his own hands. When he moves wisely he can move forward. When he does not, he will have cause to retrace and redraw his steps. Ultimately the speed and method he chooses are up to him.

The things we endure are unique to the life that we have. No two people will need the same from the day or the problem they are experiencing.

Just for today, pay close attention to the details of your own business. See what situations you are presented with and what they are trying to teach you. Allow others the benefit of your attention when appropriate but allow them also the opportunity to work through their own stuff. The lessons behind their problem might not be the same as yours, but the solution will give what is necessary – tenfold.

32

❖❖❖

I will stand by my words.

In the course of a day, millions of words fall from our lips. The thoughts we think and the links we form are too many to contemplate in the space of one moment. We talk from morning till night about anything and everything. Words are the currency of the soul.

Words we utter depend on the mood and the topic of our time, but do we always say what we mean or mean what we say? Sometimes we speak to keep the peace, sometimes to hurt or to prove a point and even to manipulate a situation for a specific outcome. Words are used readily without thought of their content or effect.

The language we speak has many forms but words become daggers and arrows as well as kindness and love. They are energy in motion: Energy that has been born to the physical by our utterance – by our free will. They are bricks that we build our life upon.

Just for today, notice the words you use and the way you choose to use them. Notice whether they carry a positive or negative charge to their destination and try to limit your lips to the ones you would be proud to stand up and own.

33

◆ ◆ ◆

I will turn all my fear and negativity over to God, to Source, to recycle.

In the beginning man was in tune with his maker. He was able to speak freely of his inner thoughts, emotions and feelings. He was able to share all experiences of the things he had learnt. He was able to voice fears and happiness so well that all he was – became and remained a part of the whole.

Somewhere along the course of evolution this stopped. Man became trapped by his mind. He believed he was alone – alone with his desires and also his fears. He thought he had to struggle against all odds for survival and growth. He has been fighting that same battle ever since.

But the truth is far from this. Man is not alone and he never was. He never could be because he is part of the planet he lives upon, the body that gives him life. Man is the link that brings information back to the whole, and, as such, he cannot ever be disconnected from it. To think that we are disconnected is just illusion. Man is the relayer of living energy back to the planet itself.

Because of the role man must play in the Earth's existence, all thoughts he thinks must play their part too. Thoughts must flow freely on an even and positive keel. They allow Earth's own living energy to flow in the way that should.

Just for today, be aware of your thoughts and notice whether they are positive or negative in nature. Whether they take you forward, or hold you back.

Thought is energy in motion; so if yours do not fit the moment you experience, recycle them. Send them upstairs to Source, in silent request that they be removed and dealt with according to the needs of the moment. Ask that your mind remain focused, balanced and at peace. Let love and illumination replace worry and stress so that your day may run as smoothly as it should. Because you are not alone, know you will always be heard and aided accordingly.

34

❖❖❖

I must recycle my negativity before it takes hold somewhere and bounces back at me.

The power of thoughts we think far outreaches anything we think them to be.

Thought is energy in motion. Good balanced thoughts produce positive energy, whereas stress, worry and fear produce imbalance. They are negative. Because thoughts carry energy, all thoughts carry either a positive or negative vibration to their focal point. They feed their destination with a charge that in turn fuels the situation or person their content is about. A bad mood sends invisible sparks everywhere. Some will fade to nothing while others will add to and change the energy of other people around. They feel unnatural and uncomfortable to a usually well balanced aura.

Thoughts are energy transmitters. They should flow freely from the mind of their maker to their target. Positive thoughts send their charge sure and true. Negative ones do too but they also leave their residue with the thinker. Negative energy is heavy and its continuous bombardment upon any subject will cause a blockage to occur over time.

Just for today, notice when you feel downhearted, heavy or stressed. Notice whether your thoughts are heavy or light. Recycle any that tumble around, uncontrolled, in your mind. Recycle those that bring you pain or keep you holding on too tightly to the past, to the day before or even to the future. Let all thoughts go – except those that you know you should have right now, relating only to the moment you are in. Let your mind focus fully on your present activity or focal point.

35

❖❖❖

I must love at all times.

Love, is not just loving with the heart and the euphoria it brings, but is about being open to the truth and the light of the moment.

Love is about understanding and letting barriers go. It is about crossing bridges where before anger and resentment, fear and pain had pulled them down. Love is about living and letting others live life as they would wish to. It is non-judgemental. It is acceptance and forgiveness, sharing and letting go of painful memories and past experiences. Love is the strength that will take us beyond the turmoil of the present and the hurt of the past.

To love is not to sweep under the carpet but to see with fresh understanding. It is the ability to look at oneself and at others in the light of true sight; the ability to let bygones be done and to see each day as a new page or another chance, a new beginning with fresh opportunities to set things straight. To let go and forgive is not the same as to condone, but in the light of true understanding the past can be laid to rest and the present allowed to bloom.

Just for today, when you are sad or in pain, ask for the illumination of love to be present instead. Ask that all thoughts and feelings be gone except those that are true and correct.

36
❖❖❖

Today is a new day. All that happened yesterday should be left there.

The nature of life is that it is constantly changing. It ebbs and flows like the tide of the sea. Good and bad, sorrow and pain must all play their part even in the span of one day. They play equal roles in the course that life must run.

Because man can never be immune from life, good and bad will always intervene in his path: some of his own making and some that is not. This is the nature of life.

Every day we wake up is a new day, a new page that's been born. What we choose to do with that day and how we write upon it, is up to us. Man is the creator of his own real time life story, his own destiny, and because of this he also creates his own now.

Just for today, let go of the past. Let hurt and pain be taken away so memories can be looked at like photographs. Let past arguments lose all sting as you send affiliated attachments and feelings upstairs to Source for recycling. Just as you empty a bin, you can empty your mind of all it does not need. You choose the content of your thoughts with every one you think from now on. With the power of love and peace as your guide you have the choice of whether memories are sad or happy.

37

❖ ❖ ❖

I must keep my inner self balanced at all times.

At the beginning of time, balance was a critical factor. Things that were, worked in complete harmony with the things that were going to be.

Only now man has become out of balance, with both himself and the planet he lives and strives upon. Man is the make-or-break factor in the future of life as he knows it.

Balance is the cornerstone of life. It is the most important rule of chemistry and creation. It plays a far greater role in all that we do than we realize.

Just for today, be aware of all things in your life that require balance to help them function as they should – your mind, your work and play, your sleep pattern, your thoughts, your hopes and aspirations, your diet and your bank account. Notice the times you let any of these slip and the knock-on effect this has in other areas. Man is not a machine, but correct balance will play a huge part in finding a state happiness and peace of mind. The balance of your future relies completely on the time and effort you place upon the importance of balance today.

38

❖❖❖

I must ask for help when I need it, and recognize that help when it occurs.

Help has a different meaning for everyone. There are those who ask before they try anything themselves, because alone they feel inadequate or think that their effort will not be good enough. There are those who ask for help exactly when they need it but are then too closed in opinion to use it as it comes. Some ask from trial and error, when all they've tried has failed and yet others who allow their helper to complete the task – instead of working it out for themselves. Then there are people who ask for help from those wiser and better skilled for the job.

Help will come to all when needed – or when we ask – but the key is learning to recognize whether it is needed at all. Help is a light that shines in the dark, but when we rely too heavily on its presence we shift the weight of our own responsibility to another. Our task can quickly become their burden.

Just for today, look at the times that you ask for help and the reason you require it. Decide if you really do need it. Help must be just that – help. It must not mean a transfer of tasks from one person to another. When necessary, help will always appear – but it might not be in the form you anticipate. The universe will always come to our aid but we must be open enough to receive and recognize it when it does. Mentally send your thoughts upstairs to Source and ask for what you need.

Only you have the knowledge of the kind of help you require, so ask and watch out for the difference – as you work on.

39

❖ ❖ ❖

I must learn to take my life one step and one day at a time.

Have you ever noticed how the moment we reach a goalpost, we change it? How we run through the day as fast as we can to get to a target, which then whizzes by? Have you thought about the energy wasted on playing both past and future events over and over again in our mind, or about how things rarely turn out the way we imagine them at all?

Each time we get fearful, stressed or over excited in any way about future situations or events, we place our present charge of mind energy straight at the point of what we were thinking about. With fear we dread the advancing day more as it starts to arrive, because we also feel the extra negativity we have channeled with our thoughts into the event, situation, person or place itself. With overexcitement and anticipation the opposite is true as we place too much hype up ahead, so when the time comes along it can hardly match the opinion of how we thought it would be.

Just for today, try to remain purely in the moment at hand. When pre-planning is necessary remain balanced and open to the things you must do. Allow the day to creep forward as it will, completely fresh and unencumbered without unnecessary anticipation. Each day and each moment is an experience within its own right – so enjoy it as it was intended to be.

40

❖ ❖ ❖

I will take each moment as it comes. Worry comes from pre-empting these events and trying to fit them together before their time.

Worry is the biggest cause of illness and death in the world today. How many of us can place a hand on our heart and say that we don't worry? Even the highest, most enlightened being is prone to this behavioural habit, and without being aware that we can stop ourselves, we never shall.

Worry is a fear-based thought that will dominate our consciousness as long as we allow it to continue. Worry begets more worry. It brings loss of sleep and eats away at peace of mind until we can think of nothing else. We talk to our friends and hope that they can lighten the issue but often we walk away as encumbered as before. Yet there is another alternative. How many times have we said even to ourselves, 'Why did I worry at all? The thing was not as bad as I thought it would be'?

Just for today, when you notice your thoughts in a state of worry, stop them and bring them back to the moment at hand. Send your thoughts upstairs to Source for recycling, so that all you no longer need is removed. Ask for the answers you need to be given and that you may be conscious of this help at the appropriate time. You can do this as often in the day as is necessary until your mind gets the message that you do not want worry anymore. Until you consciously break the cycle you will always get what you have always got. Worry!

41

◆ ◆ ◆

I must allow myself to take time out when I need it.

Man is like a computer. He is the product of all he has been programmed with. He is a work in constant progress.

During the course that a life will take we learn to do many things. We learn to do them well or to simply get by, by achieving the minimum that we have to. We do so much automatically that we hardly pay attention to the use of our energy or time at all. We cram as much as possible into a day, become stressed when we don't reach our targets; yet how realistic are we with the expectations we have placed upon ourselves? How often do we try to overstretch our capabilities or the allotted time we have available? How often do others demand more than we can reasonably deliver and again how often does our heart want to help them, with disregard to the excess demands we place on our already overfilled day?

Just for today, take a look at the demands you are subjected to. Take a look at the way you expect time to work and whether you spend it wisely or allow it to drain away untapped. Are you fair with yourself and with others and are they as fair with you? Your inner being already knows, so listen to the truths it is telling you.

42

♦♦♦

I must listen carefully to others.

Daily we are bombarded with the sounds of life: nature, the banter of people, television, stereos, cars, industry; these are to list but a few. We hear the hum of our thoughts and our blood as it courses through our veins. There is so much background noise that when silence finally arrives we hear a high-pitched whistle before we finally get used to the stillness.

Yet how many of us consciously listen? How often do we hear the sounds and the words purposely directed at us?

Just for today, let your mind be still and your ears open. Hear the words that are being said to you. Give those around your complete attention when they speak. Allow yourself the opportunity to listen carefully to the things that you need to hear.

43

♦♦♦

I must use each and everyday to its fullest.

Time is man's most precious commodity. Once spent, it can never be regained, yet man lets it dwindle away without even consciously realizing.

Time exists only on Earth. It has no meaning except to man, so this sets him apart from the animal species. It matters how we spend time and it matters how it is harnessed for our own personal use. The time allotted to each life is but a drop in the ocean of this world's existence, yet in the short space man has been part of it, his presence will never be removed. It is clear he has been here and also that he will leave his mark for generations to come.

Just for today, be aware of how you spend your time and enjoy this precious gift for the treasure it really is. Be proud when you look back at the end of your day, and sure that you used it to its fullest, not just in work but in love and enjoyment as well. Use this day as though it were your last and tie up any loose ends.

44

❖❖❖

I might not always be happy to speak my truth but it always needs to be spoken.

Truth. What does that mean?

Truth is that which stands alone and cannot be altered. It is the true picture. No amount of explanation, coloration or illusion can change it. No word can be spoken that can alter its existence in any way. Truth can be our strongest ally when we stick by it and it can be our worst enemy when we don't.

Truth exists all around us in everything, but the truth that affects us most is the version we carry within our own head. It affects all that we think, do and say. It affects our interaction with the life we live and the way we live it. A common block in man's life is miscommunication and this often stems from misunderstanding in the way we think and the way we interpret the truth that we see.

Just for today, look at the way that you view each experience you have. Do you see it as it really is or do you see through the eyes of your emotions? Truth has no emotion. It simply is – as all that it is.

45

❖❖❖

I must stand firm and stand tall, but always with kindness and love.

Thoughts have many directions. They are what life is based upon. They are the foundation stones to character, hopes, fears, achievements and failings. The thoughts we have about ourselves determine whether we are shy or out going, passive or prominent. The way we view others has the same influencing effect because we feed the way they then view themselves.

How we think and then react will always have influence somewhere. In a peaceful state of mind we can influence with kindness and love but when we are rattled and stressed, we send anger and turmoil in every direction. We ruin a perfectly normal day in seconds with words too hastily conveyed.

Just for today, be aware of every word that you dish out. Notice the effect your words have both on others and your own peace of mind. It is important you speak your truth but do it without undue emphasis or innuendo. Try to be as innocent and as unattached to a particular outcome as possible.

46

❖❖❖

I must keep my head in the stars but my feet on the ground at all times.

Thoughts we have and things we say and do reflect the type of people we are and would become. Yet how often do we monitor their content?

Life is like a computer program, with each event and thought subject leading to another. Every deed we undertake and the choices we make take us one step closer to the next. We alone shape and mould the course that our life will follow. We are the creators of the world that we perceive and not the victims of circumstance we often believe we are. Yes, life does inevitably deal its blows but how we choose to overcome them to go forward is entirely our own affair.

Just for today, keep your feet firmly planted on the ground and focus only on the moment you are experiencing. Take it for its true worth but keep your mind at its highest potential. Don't underestimate your own ability and keep your intentions as honourable as you know they should be. Ask that all illusion and negativity be recycled, that your day can flow as it should.

47

❖❖❖

I must go with the flow of the day as often as I can.

The day you are in is a new day, a blank page that as yet is unwritten. You will write upon it yourself with all that you say, do and intend.

Appointments, meetings, work and chores are all normal things of life, but sometimes we can make them too rigid. We become bound by them and by the hands of the clock, until we cannot move left or right without fear of failing to achieve their fulfilment. Yet this need not always be so. We have merely conditioned ourselves to this programming. Life itself is intended to flow.

Just for today, be like the willow and bend a little. When the day throws an unexpected twist, go with it instead of against it. The chances are that you still will achieve all you intend but in an altered order. You may even obtain a little unexpected fun!

48

❖❖❖

I must learn that I have a voice too. I must not become a victim of the thoughtlessness of others.

The voice you have is yours. It is your unique mode of communication.

Freedom of speech is now the gift we enjoy as a product of

the efforts of our ancestors. We live at a time that allows us to do and say whatever we want. No one can punish us for being our true selves (at least this is so in the West). No one can tell us how to think or behave. We are the very canvas of the pictures we wish to paint and in doing so move forward in the life that we live.

Yet sometimes we give all this freedom away. We allow others to call the tune to which we dance. We let them pull our strings and then resent them for doing it, when really it is we that allow this to happen, and probably have done so since a very early age. For many, this has become a part of their normal pattern of existence.

Just for today, take your own power back. You are the only one to know how you feel and also what you need to be doing. Ask that your aura can be as small as it can be – and for anyone you interact with to be the same. You are valuable because you are unique. Your lifelong experiences have made you so. Your truth is as valuable as anyone's. Take the time to voice it.

49

❖ ❖ ❖

I must do what I need to do, when I need to do it.

Life must ebb and flow. There are distinctly times to move forward and also times to stand and wait, but the trick is to recognize the difference.

Man has become locked in a train of thought that he is alone and must fight his way through life for all his needs, but this is not the truth. Each person is born with a designated guardian that stands at his left side through the whole of his life. Belief is not necessary, nor will things alter, for this truth is simply the truth.

Man is not alone. He is a part of a greater whole. This is a truth he does not always yet know. Many unseen forces try to help and slot into place the things that man needs the most.

Just for today, try to go with the flow. Do what you must at the time it must be done but leave room for the unexpected to slip in when necessary. It is at precisely these times your invisible help can be given.

50
❖❖❖

I am allowed to do things for me as well.

It is the nature of man to try to please, not just for others but to feel good inside himself.

We learn to react and interact with life through the people around us when we are young and impressionable. We learn what brings us trouble and also what brings us praise and keeps us happy. We learn that pleasing others gives us a pleasing feeling too. We are encouraged to place the needs of family and friends before our own, but sometimes we can learn this too well. When the time we have left is too sparse, we can forget about our own needs entirely.

Just for today, notice when you forget your own self. Take a little time out here and there when you need to and take care of the things that crop up. Life is supposed to be fun, so when things get too heavy for too long, readjust the load and be kind to you. Move with a spring instead of a limp.

51

❖❖❖

I will not feel guilty today.

We have a talent for feeling bad about things we have no control over at all.

The Bible depicted the first sin in the Garden of Eden and since then we have carried the burden of the world upon our shoulders. We invite guilt when really we have nothing to feel bad about. Man is responsible for his own life and for his own actions. He is the only one to decide what to do with them. Mistakes he made in the past, even yesterday, must be laid aside. He is given a new chance everyday to set the record straight and become a better person. He alone must decide that he really wants this and the rest will follow just as surely as night follows day. He is the creator of his own destiny – at all times.

Just for today, ask that all negativity and unnecessary guilt be recycled. The choices you took yesterday were right for you at that time, or you would not have made them. Any guilt that you now feel, you placed there yourself after the said time of event. Send your thoughts upstairs and ask that you may be shown the most appropriate way to move forward from here. Stay in the light and the love of all you know to be true and correct until slowly you become the best version of the self you always wanted to be.

52
❖❖❖

I will ask to be healed.

The many worries and troubles that man carries with him are the cause of his ill health, his fatigue, stress and depression. They are the link between his fear and his failings.

Man is both a physical and an energy being. The two must exist in complete balance to maintain a happy state of health and wellbeing. Yet to attain this, man must first do some work on knowing his inner self. He must understand how he subconsciously adds to his troubles in the course of his normal daily life. He must be able to let his past rest and the future come forward unhindered. He must be fully functional in his present, to allow the flow of his life to connect as it should.

At the root of man lies the instinct to take control of all he will become, but not in the way that he thinks he must. The life he has is his to live but he also has access to help and this he must understand. He has not been left alone to struggle and fend for himself in an unkind world, but instead he is the one that leads the way. Man creates his own reality with every thought and word he chooses to put into play.

Just for today, ask that you can be healed from the wounds you have collected and carried through the course your life has taken.

(I am I) The time has come to let go. Ask for the healing you need. Ask for old pain and guilt to be gone. Ask for illusion to fall away. Ask that you be open to receive the day you are in as you should, and that love and peace be your guide. Ask and you will be given. That is my pledge now to you. (I am I)

53
◆◆◆

I may be asked my opinion and it is fine to share it.

Along the course of life people ask for our opinion but the words we share must be our own truth. There may be times we would rather not get involved but the words must be spoken just the same.

Every person lives his own unique experience, based on the route that his life will follow, but now and again it is necessary to highlight things to help someone else. Sharing your own experience is not telling someone how to live and what they should do next. Your truth will always have value when you share it as it really is.

Just for today, when you are asked for your opinion share it honestly and openly. Speak only from your own experience.

54

❖❖❖

I must ask for extra energy as and when I need it.

Energy is the life force of the planet. It must flow through man freely and uninterrupted.

Energy is moved from person to person with every thought, action and deed we make. Conversation is energy transference from one person to another. The purpose of man, other than to live his life's experience, is that he is a channel for Earth's energy to flow through.

Man is responsible for keeping his own channel clear and uninterrupted. During life, stress and problems can clog his channels. He can become blocked to the point of becoming ill.

Just for today, ask that you can be healed. Ask to become a free and open vessel for the Earth's vital energy to flow through. Allow stress and illusion to be removed from your being just as soon as they occur. Ask to be firmly rooted in the day you are in, that you can receive all the energy you need to see you easily through to its end.

55

♦♦♦

I must remember those less fortunate than myself.

The life that is given is man's to use at will. All possibilities are open to all who will grasp them but man limits his potential with the walls and boundaries he places himself within.

In the beginning all men were the same. Today we are still born equally but into different circumstances and lifestyles. The Earth's population has never been so diverse but the heights a person can attain are endless. There is nothing that cannot be achieved when our minds are put to work, yet we live in constant illusion, pain and doubt. We are the ones who limit our own potential – not God and not the universe.

Man can rise above his limitations but only when he has access to the means and tools to do so. Because he views his world through the vision of his present fear and turmoil, he can miss the trigger points that life puts in his path to help. He can remain in limbo, being neither happy nor optimistic, for years.

Just for today, ask that all illusion be lifted and recycled, that you can move forward in the truth and light of the day at hand. Ask that you can see the reality that exists in all things, instead of the image that is often portrayed. The universe will forget no man, but it needs the help of all – to put things back to the order they must be.

56

❖ ❖ ❖

I must focus on the task at hand and on nothing else until it is done.

Man is busier today than ever before. Yes, his predecessors were busy, but in a different way. For them life was manually harder than the majority can imagine.

Time is precious. Life is demanding. Man earns more but he works to produce more, both mentally and physically. High expectations, quantity, quality and speed are demanded from everywhere. He is caught in the loop of demand and he even demands of himself.

The need to multitask is great and the use for automatic pilot has rocketed. Man does much that he does without thought of whether it is necessary or not.

Just for today, remain focused on the things that you do. Complete one task at one time and in turn give it your fullest attention. Only then can you curb unreasonable levels of demand made of you.

57

❖ ❖ ❖

I must not fear at any time.

Fear is a negative emotion that has little value when it exists. It stems from thoughts that automatically link back to similar occasions, when you were hurt or down, emotionally or physically, by your own action or by another's. It pulls old, past, fear-driven feelings forward into the present.

Every day is a new day. Its blank page waits for instruction. How can we know in advance how an occasion will be, when as yet it has still not been experienced? A similar occasion may be completely different to past experience. Being fearful attaches negative energy to a forth ,coming event with every thought we produce in advance, until really we do not want it to come, yet often things are not as anticipated.

Just for today, maintain a relaxed and open approach to life. Notice when you dread the future, whether it is a meeting today or something in weeks to come. Ask that your energy body remain as small as a grain of sand and that any negativity you cause be recycled. Ask that all your interactions may be as they should be – unwritten.

58

❖❖❖

Only two trains of thought exist – fear and love. All others are offshoots from these.

Yet life is even simpler than that. Love is positive (or good). Fear is negative (or bad).

Love is balanced. It is pure and true. When we operate from within its boundary we have peace of mind and an open, giving outlook. We can breeze through life lightly and easily. Problems seem to melt and disappear and even those we must attend to go quickly and without excess fuss. People smile, colours look bright and we are happy to be a part of the world. In fact, we are happy to be alive and with life.

Fear is out of balance. It is the product of illusion and presumption. It comes from looking too far into an unwritten future or from looking in too blinkered a way at the past. Fear keeps us bound in its chains until it drives us mad. It can ruin a moment, the day you are in or even your lifetime when it is allowed to rampage and take root. Fear is an ego-based emotion that does nothing but prevent us from growing. It is the root cause of illness, mistrust, misunderstanding and decay. It stops the very flow of life that must course through man unhampered.

Just for today, be aware from which mode of thought you operate. Notice whether you are open or closed, happy or sad. Let your mind be free of the past and solely in the present. Let the power of the universe uplift and guide you for the whole of your day. You create your reality through the thoughts that course through your mind.

59

♦♦♦

I must help to light up the corner of the world that I live in.

Jesus said, 'I am the light of the world. All that follow me will become the light and will be received by God.'

The Bible is a book. It depicts a time when story and fable were the news and film of today. There was no television, nonewspaper and no automated communication system. All teachings were handed down by either word of mouth or the replay of true events in fable form.

Jesus was a man; a man of flesh and blood just like us, but at the extreme 'good' end of the spectrum, in behaviour and ability. We are not so good. Yet we are still the same as he. Inside all is the ability to be good, to do good and to heal. Inside all is the ability to become the highest version of the self we would be. Yes, today we are more materialistic, but this is not necessarily bad. We just live in an age where we are able to live in comfort and have nice things. We live in a time where our desires are easily met, yet this is also our downfall. We think we can better ourselves through the quality of belongings and status.

Yet it is the man that matters, not his possessions or status. It is the thoughts we think, the words we use and the actions we make. Possessions bring comfort and for a while can feel good, but eventually enough is enough.

Just for today, notice from where you operate. Does your life revolve around your material wealth or from the light of the person within? Do you operate from a sense of the self or from the view of a greater world perspective? Silently raise your thoughts and ask for the truth that you need. The light that is you is waiting to shine. Don't cloud it with unnecessary clutter.

60

❖❖❖

I must make up my own mind.

The life we have is our own to live. We are solely responsible for all it will be. We have the right to make it work in any way we choose, but there is the catch – we must choose it.

Man is the product of every choice and decision he has made.He makes every choice to his highest ability, to reach his target or to make him happy, yet how often is he happy in his daily life?

Just for today, be aware of the choices you make. You are creating your life with your now. Move in small steps. Take charge of your own life. Don't feel pressured by others but be open to the complete truth of the moment. Be free to sit tight until you completely know which option to take, and be honest with yourself and your thinking. You must make up your own mind. No one else has the key to do it for you.

61

◆◆◆

I must not take another's mood on board as my own.

We are daily invisibly bombarded by energy vibrations that exist all about us. These vibrations are made by the thoughts and emotions of people and are a natural by-product that is vital to the Earth we live upon.

When we are happy, we are uplifted and uplifting. We carry a positive charge to our energy that then connects and becomes larger as it intermingles with other positive people around. Like attracts like and we have a great day. The life force that we need can flow freely through us all as it should. On the other hand, the opposite occurs when we are mad or in a stressed mood. By being negative our negative energy stays with us. It hangs about like a cloud and sticks like glue to our being. Like attracts like once more and negative vibes pass in every direction that they are sent to by action or thought. Our system is blocked and we can find it hard to shake ourselves free.

Just for today, notice when you feel gloomy or stressed. Notice the telltale heaviness which lies like a lump in your chest, your stomach or your neck. Silently send up your thoughts and ask that this negative energy be removed and recycled, even though at this point you might not know the cause. Silently ask the same for others around, when you notice them in a negative state, and wait patiently for the difference to take hold. You are the one to choose whether you will be in a positive or negative state of mind for the day and you also have the choice of whether you accept another's mood to add to your own.

62

❖ ❖ ❖

I will learn to live as happily as I deserve.

Life is for living. It is by our own choice that we are here and by that same choice we play the part we do in the life role we have carved for ourselves. It is also by our choice that we shall carry on to become the person we will be during the span of this life.

Man is separated from all other species by a conscious mind that can know itself, fend for itself and know all others apart from itself. Its ability to create, experience and freely express is the gift we have been given since the time of our creation, since man first appeared on this Earth.

The true destiny of man is to experience life and this can only be achieved fully in the now. The true now can only be accessed in a state of openness and this can only be when the mind is in a state of happiness and love, when it is relaxed and at peace with itself and the world it surveys. All other emotion will alter its thoughts and the direction that you then will follow, and when this occurs you have lost your control. Your mind instead will be at the mercy of those emotions' themselves.

Just for today, flow with the life force that takes you most directly towards your true purpose, allowing your day to unfold as it will and go with it. You may be pleasantly surprised.

63

❖❖❖

I must realize that most things that bug me are not directed personally to me but are experienced by everyone, every day.

If life was a constant bed of roses, how could we ever know the difference between sadness and happiness? How could we ever grow and how could we know the bliss of reaching the next objective?

Life must flow and ebb – like the oceans of the world. There are times to move forward, when all things fall into place, and there are equally times we must stand still to wait or take stock. Even nature has times she must stand still, to retrieve and conserve her reserves before bursting forward once more in the spring.

Just for today, notice what life is saying to you. Allow its subtle lessons to propel you forward or to hold you safely where you are for a while. When little things annoy you, take a different look at the meanings they carry and allow yourself the help of the answers you will receive.

64

❖ ❖ ❖

I must live with the flow of life.

Time is our most precious commodity, yet often we try to make it go faster. How often do we let our mind wallow in the past without giving a second thought to the moment we are in? How often do we wish we were already in the future, somewhere, anywhere, other than the place we are in right now?

When we are young we are empty vessels, devoid of direction but full of vitality and wonder and life. As we grow we become focused: focused on learning and experiencing all that life offers. Then we mature. Like the summer, we blossom and bloom and show our bright colours. We live the life that we have chosen to live. We fruit and make ready for the autumn of our years; but do we consider enough the time spent in our now? The time we have just to be? Instead all too oftenwe do what we do simply because we have set in that mould.

Life is not a chore. It is not cast in stone. You must allow it to flow as it must. The whole of the world is your oyster. Life is all you can want it to be. Let go of the chains that hold you rigid. Be spontaneous and do something just because you would like to. Experience the fun and be like the child at the brink of the rest of his or her life.

Just for today, go with the flow.

65

❖ ❖ ❖

I must keep my corner of the world in check. I must pull in the reins when necessary and keep my own space clutter-free.

Each person is the centre of his or her own universe. The life we live and experience begins with us, with our own self. By our interaction and effort we have total freedom and control over all that we do and of the self we want to portray. We have the power to choose with every tick of the passage of time. We set the scenethat we then take part in. We alone choose who we will be and then how to react to life as it comes.

Man is like a sophisticated program. All variable options are open to him depending on the next move he wishes to make. We establish that link for ourselves, with action or non-action, thought, word and deed.

Intention and thought content mean everything here. They are invisible instructions that we send out for life and for others to follow. They are the next moves we intend life to take.

Just for today, be aware of the way you plan out your day. You are in charge of your choices, your intention and your interaction with others. Be careful to stay completely in the now you are in. Now is the place that should be held firm like the reins of a free-spirited pony. Don't let your thoughts run away. Remain in the truth and recycle all illusion. Know where you wish to go and take the straightest route. Remain focused yet flexible in all interactions, and experience the day as it comes.

66

❖ ❖ ❖

I must always follow my heart in things that I do.

To follow the heart is to enjoy the things that you do. Life has many automatics. We get up, we wash, we eat and we go to work. We come home, we relax or go out. The intervals between offer room for more automatic, but necessary, activity.

Just for today, let go of the grip a little. Allow yourself to take note of the things you can take for granted. The true life is waiting for an opportunity to come through. All you must do is let it.

67

❖ ❖ ❖

I must listen to my instincts.

Man is equipped with many talents. He has the power to think and to choose for himself. He has learnt through life to read and to reach for anything he desires, to interact with the world and to put into place the necessary stages that will lead him towards his destination. He plays people and situations to the best of his advantage.

Very often we hear only the loudest voices both outside and in our own head. We listen to things we most want to hear, things that agree with our own train of thinking, yet often we should listen to a quieter voice, to that of our own conscious instinct.

Just for today, listen to your second thoughts. Find out why you have doubts and check to see if they are justified. Your instinct will help you choose and re-choose until you are completely happy with the situation. If your doubts remain and there is no obvious justification, ask silently that they be recycled. Ask for peace and balance to be restored and ask for some help to take you safely forward.

68
❖ ❖ ❖

I must allow myself to be human and therefore sometimes fallible.

Only man has ability to expand beyond limitations placed upon him at birth. The world has no barriers that man is unable to overcome. He exceeds everything he can imagine. He is his own creator and also his own judge. Man is bound only by laws of good conduct and by the boundaries in place in his mind. Whatever he can imagine today, he can gain the ability to be.

Yet for all his intelligence, man can sometimes forget he is only human and it is his nature to make mistakes and get things wrong. Once he has learnt any task, he can forget that more learning still needs to be done. He forgets that another angle or point of view could exist.

Just for today, remember that you are a human being. Remember it is human nature to sometimes get things wrong. A mistake is not the end of the world but another chance to grow beyond the place you are now at.

69

❖❖❖

I must listen to the advice I ask for.

When we are young we are programmed to learn. Like sponges we soak up and store all that we come across until a time we can do something with it.

Adults can be the reverse. Many of us think we know best about many things and we proudly parade that to anyone caring to listen. Often this is fine. It is how things should be. The people we know communicate also in the same manner. It is a form of sideways growth, where each person will help another in his vicinity to grow.

Just for today, be aware of advice you get when you say you are stuck. Listen carefully to words that are given, but choose wisely whether they will serve or whether you must search more widely and choose another option. Remember that what works well for one might not necessarily be what another is in need sof. We are all travelling along our own path.

70

❖❖❖

I must take my time to do the things that need to be done.

The course of any day is naturally busy. We try our best to squeeze in all that we can, but to compensate we can be lazy. Because we work so hard, we feel more than justified to do nothing at all when we can. This is fine when it serves the purpose of rest but in itself is a state of imbalance. As the pendulum of life swings too far over one way it must also come back, swinging also too far, in the opposite direction to compensate. The reality and balance of life should be different.

Balance is a place of existence somewhere between the two. The world about us lacks balance and that in turn filters right back to us. We live in a state of imbalance that has grown to be accepted as normal. We have become over-tolerant of the out-of-balance states of our life.

Just for today, try to find the centre of balance that should exist in your day. Work at an even pace and find time to relax a little too. Find the correct time to achieve all that you know you must, and balance it with equal time for yourself and your family and friends. Remember that by living too heavily in one direction, you upset the natural balance of all other things around you.

71
❖❖❖

I will take the rest that my body sometimes needs.

Man tries to fit too much into a day – too often. We live at a time when speed is everything. All must be achieved as fast as humanly possible and even faster still, but the price that this is costing is not always immediately apparent.

The world we live upon is becoming exhausted. Its resources are being drained before they are able to replenish. The body we ourselves live in is also being exhausted as we push it further and further past existing energy levels. Man is working everything too hard, including his self.

Just for today, take note of the signals that your body sends out to you. Notice whether you are reasonable in your expectations or whether you have been pushing too far in any particular direction. When your body needs rest it is not kidding. It needs time to replenish its energy and vitamin levels, to serve you as you wish it would. Do not be lazy but do not ask too much of it either.

72
❖❖❖

I must tighten my purse strings for a while.

The whole of life is a package. Everything we do reflects something, and all things have a knock-on effect. The laws of cause and effect are inescapable.

Man lives a fast pace. He has become locked into patterns that he hardly sees but that the world about him reflects. Still he does not notice. Instead he works hard to fit in and compete on his own individual level. He joins the race that he naturally finds himself part of.

The life he lives is but a reflection. He must live the dream he desires but that is the problem. His desires are often way out of line with his budget capabilities. This is a time when all man's desires can be met – at any time he chooses – and that too is a problem. The art of patience and saving is almost forgotten as he borrows credit from the future to pay for his present.

Just for today, take a look at your life. Notice whether you reside within your budget or outside it. Notice whether you act on whim or impulse or actual necessity. Just for today, live within your means. Save for the future if you must but don't steal from it. Take time to balance your life and its affairs and allow the necessary corrections to be put into place.

73

❖❖❖

I must allow others to be cross when they need to be.

The laws of nature must exist in balance, as the forces of nature must also be balanced. When a pendulum swings one way, it must swing as far in the opposite direction before it eventually comes to rest. The balance of all things is necessary because only then can stability be retained.

Man has mostly lost this balance and in turn upsets much that is around him. This is not completely his fault because mistakes have been handed down and compounded through time itself, but knowing this is so is not enough. It is up to each individual to return his life and his inner state of self to an acceptable balance and therefore peace.

Many times in a day man must make choices about things he will and will not accept. Though he is not always the instigator of his experiences, he does instigate his own responsive actions. He alone decides whether he will add to a situation or allow it to pass. The ripples of others are not ours to take on board. By shouting and screaming we merely add fire to fire and here there can never be a winner.

Just for today, allow others their own space and the turbulence of their emotions. It is up to you to deal with only your own. Keep them in their own state of balance. If you make a mistake, deal with it calmly and openly. If the anger about you is nothing to do with you, then send up your thoughts and ask for it all to be recycled. Ask that illusion and negativity be replaced by truth and peace of mind.

74
❖❖❖

I must help others when they are struggling.

Man's destiny is to live and experience life in any way that his choices dictate. Each is on his own path of experience and discovery. Each will follow his own chosen route towards his eventual destination, the choice of which remains entirely within his free will.

During the course of his journey there will be straight roads and junctions. There will be fast lanes, traffic and pitfalls. The way he responds to these will depend upon the route he next wishes to take and the provisions he must put into place. His life is a reflection of his own skill and judgement until this moment in time, and the future will rest entirely upon his choosing in his now.

The place where man is now is exactly the place in which he has placed himself and it is where he needs to be to go forward; but how he deals with this place is also by freedom of choice.

Just for today, notice when someone needs help. Offer the advice they require, but allow them to make their decisions themselves. Remember that what has worked well for one will not necessarily work as well for another, and that all options must be carefully considered. The quickest solution is not always the best and a slower route could turn out to be the best option. Once a problem or lesson is correctly overcome, it is unlikely to be placed there again.

75

❖ ❖ ❖

I must be as honest in my views as I can possibly be.

The art of communication is not always as straightforward as we believe. Even simple things can be misconstrued out of all proportion because along the way they have been misunderstood entirely.

The words we use and the things we think and do are strongly dependent on our feelings and views at that time. Even the way we talk will change from person to person as we slip automatically into a pattern of behaviour comfortable for the occasion or friendship.

The people we love should know us best but they too fall into a trap of selective vision and interpretation. They see only what they want to see or, more correctly, only what we allow them to know. Over half of our personality make-up resides internally, within our own selves. Depending on moods, we can be a complete other version inside. How can others understand or relate to us correctly when they only see half of the picture?

Just for today, in your dealings try to be open and honest. Recycle unnecessary thoughts and stay in the truth of the moment. Say all that needs to be said, kindly, but without undue coloration for another's understanding or benefit. Ask with your thoughts for all you need to be given, and that truth and understanding win through.

76

❖❖❖

I must let others help me when I need help.

The nature of man is his need to be independent. This must be so for his uniqueness of spirit and adventure. The time may come, however, when we must turn to another for help or advice; but when we do, how often do we find the kind of help that we need?

Help comes in many guises and the best can be the least obvious choice. It is up to us to correctly weed out all we don't need – or which no longer serves our purpose. Don't be tempted to step sideways into the illusion of a situation or of your advisor. Instead wait until you know you have gathered all available variable options.

Just for today, when you need some help, send your thoughts upstairs for the highest good. Ask that you be shown the way suited best to your needs. Ask that all negativity and illusion be removed and that truth and light be your practical guide. Let others share their truths with you but remember that they are just helping.

77

❖ ❖ ❖

I must keep myself as small as possible when in the middle of turmoil.

When a camel train moves through the desert it will from time to time encounter a storm. These will vary in degrees of severity but the precautions taken will always be the same. The camels are tethered tightly and all other belongings are made as secure and as small as possible. It is obvious that the larger the obstruction, the more likely it will be hit and battered by the oncoming storm. The smaller the obstruction, the easier the storm will blow over its form.

Just for today, try to remain as emotionally small as you can. When you are faced with an onslaught, let it take its course and soon it will blow over. Ask silently that you be given thehelp you need to get safely back on course with your peace of mind. Ask also for the same for the other parties concerned.

78

❖ ❖ ❖

I must believe in myself.

We live in a time when we naturally require the love and acceptance of others. The opinions they hold seem important, as we have an inbuilt need to fit and belong. We are often most happy when surrounded by like-minded people, family and friends who equally feel comfortable with us. Yet this is not a true representation of life. No one can agree – totally, all the time. Life is full of many facets. People too have many facets. The combined opinion of everyone will make up a truer picture.

The truth that is yours you have gained through experience. Unless another option proves to be valid, you will remain strong in your strength of conviction.

Just for today, take notice of your own intuition. The things you need most are often placed in your consciousness at the time that they are required. Stop and take note of the little thoughts that nag the back of your mind. Believe in your own capability and go forward at this time with confidence.

79

❖❖❖

I must believe in God's lessons.

The lessons of God are all around. Not lessons that will hurt or harm, for that is not God's way. The destruction and chaos evident in the world even now is solely the effect of the behaviour of man. Man lives by his free will alone and the laws of cause and effect are inescapable.

It is the will of God that we should live and experience life individually, because, combined, we form a large part of the consciousness of the whole, of this Earth we live upon. But it is not the will of God that we feel separate, disconnected or alone. This is the error that has been handed down through generations, generations of misunderstanding and fear.

Lessons depicted in the Bible were really just the tip of the iceberg, relayed to fit the form of man's comprehension at the time that the Bible was created. They have also since been altered to fit the ego of other rewriters since the time of their historical formation.

(I am I) This is my truth. I love man. I am man and man is me. How could I ever not be a part of him when he lives upon my body; when he lives upon a life force that is me? (I am I)

Just for today, look for the love that exists in all things. Look for the truth that really is the bottom line. Notice the difference between the hand of man and his cause and effect, and then look again to find the will of God. Find the underlying love that exists in all things – always. That is where you will find your answers.

80
❖❖❖

I must clear my personal space and cupboards.

The personal space that is yours is not just your physical space of rooms and storage areas. This is but an echo, a mirror of your inner state of self – your true self.

You are an energy being first and foremost. Your body is simply the vessel that helps you during the course of this lifespan. That is why as you get older you will never feel any different. You will always feel as you felt when you were young – only less able to move as freely because your body holds you back. You are a being that is here to live and enjoy, to learn and to love. That is the true you.

Your personal space is your mind. This is the intelligent blueprint of who you really are. Only you have the ability to control it and this sometimes gets forgotten. Your mind is your contribution to the whole of humanity. It is this that integrates with life and all others you come into contact with.

Just for today, realize your own power. Realize that what you carry in your mind is your offering to society and back to life itself. Are your thoughts open and honest or are they led by your emotions and the deeds of the people around? Do your thoughts reside fully in the moment, or do they linger mainly in the past or on hopes of the future? All of life, your own especially, stems first from your own inner being. Take the time to ensure that your personal space is able to embrace life just as it unfolds, rather than being caught up in old outdated patterns.

81
❖❖❖

I must take the time of others into consideration.

Time ticks past in seconds and marches evenly on, yet no man can catch it, tame it or master it. Instead we remain its slave as we aim to use it as well as we might.

Labour-saving devices that would make our ancestors swoon are ever more forthcoming, but what do we do with the extra time that they save? Do we even manage the rest of the time we have to its best available outcome? The answer is no.

Often we don't. Often it slips through our fingers like water through a sieve.

When we learn the value of time, not in pounds and pence, but as a commodity that, once spent, will never return, we can begin to use it as we should. A lifetime of time will not be enough for us to experience all the wonders that being alive can offer.

Just for today, notice how you choose to spend the most precious gift you have – your time. Notice also how you ask or expect others to give you theirs. When you value your own time, begin to realize what a gift it is when others give you some of what they too will never get back. Take the time of others into consideration even more than you usually would.

82

❖❖❖

I will try to be patient at the failings of another.

In life we are encouraged to try all that we encounter. With practice we hope to improve our skills until improvement becomes the art of mastering.

Different people excel at different levels in different skills. Even though fundamentally we appear the same and are the same, we are also very different. Unique.

Being unique is part of what we strive to be – even in our sameness. We wear different clothes and have different hairstyles. We choose different jobs and homes and lifestyles.

We enjoy different hobbies at different levels of understanding and our mistakes are different when we make them.

Just for today, notice the differences in others as well as their sameness. When others fall down or fall short of expectations, be understanding. They are not you. You have your own way of doings things and living life, but you have your downfalls too. Be patient, kind and firm where necessary and remember that whatever you give out will always come back in one form or another – one day.

83

❖❖❖

I will keep my promises.

Life is built up of interaction. Chemicals react and interact with one another. People, plants and wildlife do the same. The planet is a ball of interacting energy and gases that exist and coexist together in unison.

Most of the time small changes within interactive movement are so slight that individually they make little difference at all, but, combined, they attract like for like and a whole new ball game begins. All kinds of things can happen, just because an innocent blip started a chain reaction.

Man and his interaction with others are little different. The words we speak and the deeds we do, though ofteninsignificant in themselves, can have a greater impact than we are often aware of. The things we do and say actually touch and affect the lives of other people even more than we are led to know.

Just for today, notice your interaction with other people and the world at large, and notice theirs with yours. Notice how often you feel let down or become stuck just because another has not delivered their end of what you were expecting. Notice how often you stand by your own word and notice the difference that you make with the things that you do.

84
❖❖❖

I must be patient with myself as well with as others.

Patience is a word not everyone likes. When we want something done, we want it to be now. When we want life to flow, we can't wait for things to come. All that we expect, we help it come faster and faster until now it's automatic and normal. It's become part of the times we are in. Technology and machines supersede anything that man can achieve by his own efforts alone. Machines are working and achieving speeds and production levels that now are a standard way of life, but this has drawbacks that few seldom think of. Errors and mistakes will come more quickly, go deeper and be harder to correct as they happen. The speed of life, while quick and handy, must be firmly anchored by the thoughts and constraints that will keep things in check. Fast is not always the best policy. The efforts of man without machines might be slower, but often they are kinder to the Earth and to the resources of the future yet to come.

Man will accomplish all that his needs can imagine but he must allow himself the patience to do so. Patience allows things to happen at the time and speed that they must. It also allows others to keep up and to catch up. It allows reserves to remain full and it helps us to slow down and wait.

Just for today, don't wish your life away; allow it to unfold as it should. Be patient with yourself when you think you are slow, and realize that the universe itself must hold you back sometimes until the time is better or right. All things happen in their own good time for all the reasons that they do.

85

❖❖❖

I must not overload my time.

Time is its own master; we are merely its keeper.

The time that we perceive is our most precious commodity. We can do with it as we please but its mastery is not always within our control. The pressures of life and the problems we have come thick and fast. We may view our priorities in one way while others and circumstance view them in completely another.

Each person is here on Earth for his own allotted time span and this dwindles away with each tick of the clock, yet how often do we consider that fact? Many of us never do.

Just for today, remain aware of the way that you use the time in your day. Try not to let it run like water down the drain. If it moves too quickly, then mentally send your thoughts upstairs.

Ask that your perception of time be slowed to the slowest pace possible. Ask that you may achieve all you desire, comfortably, within its given time frame. Ask this whenever you need to, but don't forget to allow some time in every day when you can step back from your pressures to just enjoy the beauty of life.

86

❖❖❖

I must finish one task completely at a time.

How many unfinished projects do you have?

Have you ever wondered why you feel as though you are always on catch-up? Why you feel you have always something to do, even when you have worked hard all day? Unfinished projects line up behind you and wait endlessly for the time you can complete or sort them out. And here is the key: waiting endlessly is what they are, loose ends that have no end because they have never been finished; they remain attached to your energy field until you let them go.

Energy is a precious thing. It is all around us in abundance, ready for us to tap into whenever our own reserves are low, but how many of us know how to do this? How many of us realize we can? Instead we drip already low reserves constantly away with the loose ends that we never concluded. Unfinished projects need throwing away or completing. They need closure.

Just for today, watch your energy level. Finish one task completely at a time before you move on to the next. Multitasking is a great ability, but unfinished projects will always be in the back of your mind. Ask silently for the extra energy you need to see you comfortably through the day you are in, and know that you can ask as often as you wish. Thereis no limit to the supply being offered to you.

87
❖❖❖

I must be bright in my outlook.

We create our own reality by the thoughts that we think. Thoughts are creative energy in motion and they will attach themselves or collect wherever you send them.

Bright thoughts will keep your mood uplifted. They are little rays of sunshine that punch through a heavier outlook. They will help to push away the gloom that can manifest anywhere. We all know people who are nice to be around and, if you stop to notice, these people are usually full of laughter and upliftment. They can help you replenish your batteries – even though you don't know why at the time.

Just for today, recharge your own batteries. Don't wait for others to do it for you. Instead send your thoughts upstairs and ask that any heaviness be lifted. Ask that love and light can be your shield and then notice the difference in your outlook. Transference of energy is a natural thing, but when more is needed we must ask. We must connect to the source from whence it flows, like a telephone that connects to the speaker. If we don't ask for what we need when necessary, who can help? Who can know? We must ask for the extra energy we require. We must ask from the source.

88

❖❖❖

I might not always be right – but I always do my best.

The best that I can do: what does that mean?

To do your best means that you always work to the highest level of achievement you can attain. The highest level you can attain is always for the highest good of any situation or outcome. The best you can achieve is not always situated at the top of the ladder but sometimes midway. When you aim to do your best you look truthfully at all options available. You work realistically within those parameters to attain the highest possible outcome at this moment in time. It may be that these parameters will fall short of your highest desires – but they are realistic and workable. At this time they will be the best that you are able to achieve.

Just for today, recycle all illusion and unnecessary glamour. Find your base requirements. Measure these with your abilities and resources to find your workable level. Doing your best is not overstretching but neither is it being too lean. With your thoughts, ask that you be shown the truth of the situation and the appropriate help to reach your outcome.

Doing your best is not a one-off, here-and-there attitude. It is a way of life, and with continuous practice it will become an automatic part of your behaviour.

89

❖ ❖ ❖

I must let those who care, care; and those who don't, to just be themselves.

The nature of man is fickle. His ability to love and care for his fellow human beings is dependent on his mood and whatever else is happening in his life. His ability to care is not always as unconditional as it should be.

During the course of life there are many opportunities to move forward under our own steam. We are often extremely independent as we build up our life and encounter the challenges that it will produce. There are also times when we have a need to group. This is part of man's nature, it is how we measure ourselves, our attainments and our sense of family. It is our feel-good factor that brings love, admiration and acceptance.

There are times when we just want to be part of a crowd. Anonymous but included nonetheless. There are times when we try to be the big fish, the one that others turn and look up to, and times when we want to relax and let down all our daily barriers and loads, when we simply want to relax and be ourselves within the security of belonging with family and friends.

Just for today, recognize where you are and what it is that you need. The love that is yours is always with you – even though others might not be in the right frame of mind to show it. Remember that they too have needs and that they simply might be operating from a different level at this moment. The people who care might not always be able to show you at the time you need them to, so allow them some space of their own. Instead, send your thoughts upstairs and ask that youreceive all you need right now from the source that is available to you. Ask that you can allow others to be themselves and that you can go forward in the moment as you should. With the love that you feel, ask silently that they receive exactly what they need at this time too – to pick them up and uplift them.

90

❖❖❖

I must allow my true potential to unfold.

When we are young the world is our oyster. It is full of wonder, excitement, knowledge and fun. Possibilities are endless because there are no boundaries in place to confine our mind as it searches to learn all that it can. The adult we then become uses this knowledge gained to become whatever we wish within opportunities available.

But somewhere along the course of life the channels we carve become deep and restrictive. We stick to them like glue and forget the world is still out there. We forget that we are not destined to travel endlessly within confines we first set when we were new to adulthood and to living alone. The world is still our oyster, even when we have commitments. Your mind is there to be used, for exploration and for knowledge. You are confined only by the limitations you have placed upon yourself.

Just for today, do something different. Do something that you have always wanted but never got around to do. One step will always lead to another and before long you will beexperiencing a whole new chapter in life. The place you are now is not necessarily the be-all and end-all of the place you must always stay.

91

❖❖❖

I am all that I can be – always.

The all that you can be is always the highest version of the self that you can attain. It is looking to the outcome of the actions you are to take.

Life always operates within its laws of cause and effect. Itcannot be otherwise. Each decision you make must have aconsequence somewhere, and, if not for you, then it will rest somewhere else. It is easy to look at the small picture of life, the one that surrounds and affects only you, but do we consider enough the effect on others as they take action because of our intervention? Are we fair and realistic or do we expect too much - both from life and from our own self? Each and every person has a life that is as important as your own, and even more so in their opinion. Any time that they have is precious too.

Just for today, be aware of the things you ask of others. Consider the use of their time. Think through all that you ask of yourself. Are all your actions and worrying necessary? Ask that your day be controlled or helped by your higher self for the highest good, and ask that all unnecessary interactions be removed.

92

❖❖❖

I must say no when I want to.

We live in a time when we try to do our best. We try to help others and not to make them sad. We try to give our children, family and friends all that they ask for, just because we hope to help make them happy.

The war left its survivors in a state of need. It was necessary to rebuild the countries and the damage, families and communities. The needs of all were many and, wherever possible, however possible, they were met. Children saw the heartaches of their elders and vowed they too would help. They learnt to go out and get exactly what they needed for themselves.

Yet the story today has somewhat changed. In the West we have abundance. Everything we possibly desire is within our capabilities and reach. Life has never been so good. We are reaping the benefits of the labours of our forefathers, and we have been reaping so long that now we are stuck in that pattern.

We have had the best, so we expect the best, and often nothing but more of the best will do. We see it as our right – regardless.

Just for today, be aware of your needs. Do you really need all that you think you do? Do others need all that they think? Just for today, separate your needs from your wants and your wants from your necessities. Do not be afraid to say no, either to yourself or to others around you.

93

❖❖❖

I must be patient and allow life to unfold as it will.

Life flows. It moves in circles and cycles. Nature moves itself within these laws. Man does not. He is out of sync.

Within tribal conditions, Native Americans knew how to work in harmony with the cycles and laws of nature. Nothing was ever removed without first making an offering or payment in kind. They knew the necessity of patience and waiting for the right time to come along. In India they also know the meaning of giving before receiving – the meaning of family, and of caring. They share their workloads and they share their possessions. They are primarily a peaceful people.

Just for today, be aware of the times you are too forceful or pushy to another. Notice when you have obstacles blocking your path and then ask yourself why. The universe is possibly asking that you wait for a better time to move forward. You will achieve all that you aim for because that is your choice, but sometimes you must proceed slowly, to allow the help that you need to come into place. Ask that you be given the patience and the wisdom to know when to go forward and how best to proceed. Remain as small as a grain of sand and proceed with the rest of your life in the meantime.

94

❖❖❖

I must take on board the correct advice of another.

It is very rare that someone knows everything. Most know a great deal about some chosen subjects and others have a wide range of general knowledge. Some learn a lot quite early in life, while others remain open and childlike throughout. They go through life in awe of all knowledge and their world will always be a place of wonder.

The law of problems and solutions will remain the same for all. A problem is a problem, no matter how it is presented.

Just for today, notice when you need to turn to another for advice, or even when they need to turn to you. We only turn to those we think can help us, because we know they understand or have been through something similar. It is up to you to decide whethertheir advice is sound or not and whether you can use it. Remain open in your outlook and watch carefully for the advice that you most need.

95

❖❖❖

I must not take advice as being detrimental to myself.

Advice is not always criticism. Advice can help us grow. It can awake our awareness to things we would otherwise not know. Those who advise us usually care. They care enough to pull us to the side.

Just for today, when you are given some advice, recognize it for the act of kindness and friendship it is. **If** you are not aware of a situation, how can it be bettered – often to your advantage? Voice a silent thank you to the universe.

96

❖❖❖

I must be flexible in my approach to the day in hand.

Each day we get up and get on. We know the direction we must pull in and what needs to be done to get there, but life isnot always as accommodating as that. Other people interact along the way.

Things we would like to do and things that we must do are different, but often they are placed together in our mind. We stress out when disturbed from the route that we aim to take.

People will need our attention at different times. This is the way of life. Work will always be waiting.

Just for today, separate your must-dos from your would-like-tos. As long as you achieve all that you must, the rest will be none the worse for tomorrow. When a spanner is thrown into your well-ordered plans, be aware that this might benefit you too.

97

◆ ◆ ◆

I must realize the boundaries of cause and effect.

For every action we take there is a matching reaction. Every thought we have will settle somewhere on someone orsomething. The words we speak are twofold too. As physical energy conductors they bear even more weight than our thoughts.

Thoughts and words operate from two different levels, although they do so simultaneously. Energy is the force that makes all things happen. It is the essence of all that we are. Infact, energy is responsible for life itself. It constitutes the life and the matter we live upon.

The laws of cause and effect are inescapable, and the life that we live is directly their outcome. How we use life is our own affair, because the choices we take are up to us. We are the creators of the reality we perceive. We are the ones that brought us to this point and place.

Life will follow the directions we give it. That is a universal law.

Just for today, curb your thoughts and the words you might mindlessly use. Be aware of the power you wield not only in your own life but also in and around others. You have all the tools that you need to take you anywhere you want to go. Be aware of how you wield them in your day.

98

❖ ❖ ❖

I must take each day one step at a time.

The way we spend our time is as important as the way we spend our money. In fact, it is more so. Money is the currency of the physical world we live upon, but time is the currency of the soul. It is the pacer of the whole of life.

Every day it is obvious that we have things that must be done at a certain time and in their own order. We operate according to a display of time on the clock, but do we consider that time as thoroughly as we should?

Every hour spent in a single day is an hour that can never be recovered. It is time taken from the lifespan that we own. How often does it slip through our fingers?

Just for today, consider whether your life is precious to you or not. Look at the time you have spent and realize that it slips silently away, every day. Look at your life and the order it is in. Are you proud to own up to it? Are you able to say there are no loose ends and if it were over today you could return home to your master with a clear, open conscience? Would you be pleased with the legacy you have left behind, and would you achieve all you would wish?

Every day and every hour are the most precious commodities you have in your possession. Look after them with the care, attention and love that they deserve.

99

◆◆◆

I must look for the truth at all times.

The true picture of life is not always apparent. It can be clouded in illusion and hype. It can be coloured by our emotions, expectations and false thoughts.

The feet we own should be firmly on the ground at all times. It is our Earth connection and as such will help keep us grounded and level-headed. Walking on air is more than just an expression. It means that our head is floating too high. For a time we are disconnected from reality and truth. To float is a nice sensation, but in a physical world it is unrealistic. It is no accident that we have a gravitational force to keep us pinned down to the ground and the planet's surface.

Truth relies on us being grounded. It is always the bottom line of every situation and as such will always stand firm under pressure. It cannot be altered or distorted by false impression or desire. The truth is simply what is.

Just for today, keep your head out of the clouds. Use clear thinking and look behind your first impressions. Is what you see as straightforward as you have been led to believe? Areyou seeing the true picture or the way you would like it to be? Send your thoughts silently upstairs and ask that all illusion be removed. Ask for grounding and focus. Ask that you may see this day in the light of truth and reality, then look again and notice the difference.

100

❖ ❖ ❖

I must remain free of illusion.

Every thought we think is an illusion until we make a fact, until we make it real by giving it life.

Thoughts are energy in motion. They are either positive or negative in their charge. All thoughts have the potential to become physical, but only those put into action will be born. The thoughts we produce will always go somewhere, and, like arrows, fly straight to their destination.

Few people realize the power of the thoughts they produce; they wrongly believe that what they think is their business, their own affair.

All of life stems from the power of thought. All that we experience was first a thought form in someone's mind. When we let thoughts run away with us we live in a state of illusion, a state where anything and everything is possible – because reality does not intervene to balance any wrong thinking out. We can be the hero or our own worst enemy. We can be as kind or as nasty in any situation we imagine, and we think that no one will ever know, that it does not matter, but we are wrong. It does matter very much. Energy becomes matter and the vibrations you send out in thought – go straight to the place of your thinking.

Just for today, curb your thinking. Be aware that you create your own reality and you are equally responsible for the vibrations you place upon the life of another.

(I am I). I too must help you, but before I can, you must be aware of your actions in the first place. I will recycle all that you allow me to, but first you must hand it up Me. (I am I).

101

❖❖❖

I must be busy in my day and relaxed in my night.

Life revolves around night and day. Electricity has allowed us to continue day into night, but on the whole the principle stands the same for all.

We are busy. There is not enough time in any one day to achieve all that we would like, so we learn to prioritize. Priority is good, but that too falls short when circumstance, things or other people get in the way. There is only so much time available, and nothing we can do to stretch it.

Just for today, think about what you expect from the use of your time. Ask silently that your perception of it be slowed down it its minimum. Every day should be used as though it is your last, and by doing so you will pave the way for peace and relaxation when night returns.

102

❖❖❖

**I must not be afraid to hand over to God, to Source, both
the good and the bad I need help with.**

Man has learnt that God is the father, that he must go to
church to give praise and thanks, but that on the whole he is
alone. He often wonders if there's no God – because if there
was, then how could he allow all he does? Surely a good, kind,
loving God would not allow all the hurt, the pain, the sadness
and the violence? He would not stand by and watch all the
flooding, the earthquakes and disasters? How are we to
believe in a God that plays games, that has favourites and
teaches us lessons? How can we believe in a God that knows
our sadness and struggle, but does not stop more from
coming on top? How can we believe in a plan, already written,
in which we must play this sad part?

All the above are the cause of man. They are the outcome of
intention, of choice and free will, of the life we live and the
energy vibrations that we transmit. Man does not realize the
power he wealds, himself, everyday, by his actions, words,
thoughts and deeds. By his anger, stress, worry and depression.

Just for today, hand all that you can, in your thoughts, back to
God, to Source. Ask that you be given focus for the task in
hand, peace for your mind and love about your person. Hand
all that you can to the power that will help you.

*(I am I). I do not wait for you to worship. I do not want your
worship. Your offering to me is your energy, your life, your
thoughts, your hopes, dreams, desires, your love. My offering
to you is my help, my love, my life. I must wait patiently by your*

side until you realize I am here, and only when you allow it can I step in. You are the creator of life. You have the gift of free will. Any interference would invalidate the very thing that makes you you. I must wait until you understand that you have only to ask, and that you never have been and never will be alone. (I am I).

103

❖❖❖

I must help all those around me grow forward.

There is more to being related than living of the same family and the same blood. Man by his very nature is connected with others and interconnected to the planet as a whole.

The growth of man requires food of mind as well as food of body. There is no time that he can say he knows everything. The universe's vast expanse will take many lifetimes to understand, but ultimately understand it man will.

As we reach out to interact, communicate and help each other, we take a sideways step. We pull others up to our level of understanding and they do the same thing for us. That is the way it should be.

Just for today, be aware of your conversation. The help that someone needs could well come from you. Speak your truth and be open. Ask silently that the words they most need may be given and then stand back and let go.

104

❖ ❖ ❖

I must pass all negativity to my father to deal with on my behalf.

The very nature of life is both good and bad, positive and negative, birth and decay.

The life that we experience relies on our sense of self-worth and fulfilment. We aim to be happy and to feel good. We like to measure the value of things we expect in terms of how they make us feel and the way we are perceived.

But life cannot always be nice. It cannot always go our way, nor should it try to. From every wrong turn we are closer to the right one. With every mistake a whole batch of lessons and pointers are born. How could we know the value of happiness if we did not know the lows that also exist? Both happiness and sadness, good and bad are equal parts of life. They both come in dribs and drabs, sometimes more and sometimes less, but they are necessary to propel us forward, and take the next step – or we would simply stand still and be stagnant.

Just for today, be aware of the times you feel low. Be aware of the moods of all others as they come to connect with you or cross over your lifeline. The positive vibrations are great but the lows must be dealt with swiftly and surely before they take hold. As you notice negativity, send your thoughts silently out to Source and ask that it can be recycled, for the highest good. Ask that it be replaced by truth and love and that you have nothing but that which you need to guide you on.

105

❖ ❖ ❖

It is not our personal gifts that determine who we are but our free choices.

The gifts we are born with are exactly that – gifts. They are often abilities that you have mastered in a past life experience, or they could even be the talents of a lifelong guide that has agreed to work with and through you in this incarnation. All gifts are for the benefit of the whole – not just for individual enjoyment. They are to be used to their highest ability – for their highest good.

We have free choice and free reign over every move we make. The version of the self that we present must always be the best we aim to be. We are the whole package of every aspect of our personality and character. Nothing can be hidden because no place exists in which to hide it.

Just for today, take a look at your true self. Notice the talents you have and how you use them. Take notice of the things that you take for granted and of things that draw others close to you. Man is not alone, he is one part of a team and each is connected to the whole – to the all that is. Each person has his own abilities and talents. Each must use them in service of some kind, to help mankind – each in his own manner and way.

106

◆◆◆

I must recognize and recycle unnecessary fear at all times.

The mind that is yours is yours to control. It never has control over you unless you let it.

Everybody's mind is individual. Each has capabilities of its own. Yet how often do we consciously make use of its strengths?

We are writing the book of our own real time life story. Each new day is a clean, blank page. Nothing is written upon it until we begin to move, to talk, to think and to act as we awake. We alone have the choice of how it will develop or pan out. The highs and the lows we can change. Any truth that we live is our choice.

Just for today, notice whether you are happy or sad, worried and stressed, or balanced, at ease and at peace. When the thoughts you produce start to carry you away, bring them back. When they are counterproductive or negative, send them silently up to the God mind, to Source, for recycling. Ask that peace, truth and balance be yours until you're happy. The finished product of this day you'll script and write is up to you.

107

❖❖❖

I must keep my emotions within their limitations of the moment that I am experiencing.

We are led by our emotions in the now we are experiencing. We pull emotions of past events forward, to tarnish our mood and the thoughts that we think. Each time we replay the past, we feed it with new energy and keep it alive. We forget that the day we are in is brand new and as yet remains unwritten, and all outcomes are possible. We forget that day to day, people and situations change. We also forget we are human and the nature of being human means mistakes are going to be made. Emotions are only useful to us when we are balanced and in order with life, otherwise they can overrule our rational pattern of thinking and lead us astray.

Just for today, be aware of your own state of peace. When you operate from within it you will let nothing shake you up. You allow others to come and go as they choose and you will notice signs of fluctuation that occur from time to time. When they do, simply recycle the emotions that do not fit and ask for peace and balance to return. Remember, happiness is a state of mind and it is available for you to choose at any time.

108

❖❖❖

I must stand straight and tall in the face of adversity and anger.

The thoughts that we think bring life to the memories we activate. We are consciously moving, evolving, biochemical and genetic machines. We take part in a story of life we choose to unfold.

Life is neither good nor bad, black nor white, neither all happiness nor all pain. It is seen according to the emotional highs and lows we experience in any one time frame. We can go from being ecstatic to despairing within moments. We react and interact to life on a moment-by-moment exchange. We let emotions rule our thinking and our thoughts then colour any trust we have of the future.

Few people realize they co-instigate many of their lifetime experiences. Others do throw spanners in our path. Life is not completely smooth for anyone, but it is up to us to choose how we take the next step forward. We can either add to the anger and confusion of a moment, or step back and wait a while for things to calm down. Highly charged emotions take time to dissipate, but they will. Direct communication after the fact will allow you to see where the breakdown actually occurred. It will offer you the chance to put it right.

Just for today, add nothing to a negative situation. Remain small in your energy field and allow the fluctuation to pass. Feelings must be aired before you can operate from a cleaner viewpoint. The way you choose to go forward is really up to you.

109

❖❖❖

I choose whether I shall be happy or sad.

Many of life's choices are taken easily and for granted. They become automatic as we use them daily within busy schedules and routines, but how many of us stop to think about the things we choose at all?

Life is an open book. The things we do to fill it is the individual side of us.

Just for today, think about your mood. Notice how you feel and why. The good mood of the moment is the future in the now. Positive vibrations reign high. When vibrations take a dive, again find out why. Check the thoughts you had – or the effects of the mood of others. Silently recycle, on their behalf and yours, any negative vibrations that may have surfaced. You have the ability to create and retain peace of mind in this moment.

110

❖❖❖

I must help others to overcome their fears.

Fears are limitations. They are barriers and beliefs, often placed upon us in childhood, to keep us safe from venturing too far in harmful directions. Sometimes they are fears of others that we have taken to mind as our own, or even left over traumas from past or present life.

To know your limits is a good thing. To know yourself so well as to know you would really not like to do something and know the reason behind it, is even better. But when your fears stop your growth or prevent you from experiencing the full freedom of life, then these are barriers that need to fall down.

To have a fear of something is a very real emotion. It can hold someone back so much that they will experience real panic and distress, and in extreme cases even death. A presence of fear is the growth of negative emotions, placed upon a particular subject every time it is thought of. Negativity is built so high that the thinker cannot see the way beyond.

Just for today, notice any telltale knots in your stomach, chest, or neck, which highlight to you that you are fearful. Notice the signals that your body sends out when you expect trouble. Notice all familiar triggers and then send them out in thought form upstairs to Source. Ask that all your symptoms can be lifted. If necessary, sit down and balance yourself. Take a few deep breaths and actually allow them to reach to the tips of your toes. Exhale slowly and ask for all unnecessary fear and negativity to be removed. Ask for balance and an open, peaceful mind. Ask as often as you need to, either for yourself or for another. Fear is looking too darkly to a yet unwritten future. Help yourself and learn to lighten up.

111

❖ ❖ ❖

I must let my true thoughts come to the fore of my mind.

Each day hundreds of thought combinations tumble through

our mind. Many chatter aimlessly without conscious recognition while others shout their content even as we try to raise ourselves above them.

The content of the mind is the difference between internal peace and war. Apart from the obvious, things to be remembered, the arena of the mind should be clear and clutter-free.

The content of your mind is also your offering to the universal consciousness itself.

Just for today, clear away the thoughts that whirl around your head. Let all but what is needed be recycled. Focus completely on the project now at hand until you decide to move on to another. Your mind will give you what it always has unless you consciously change the rules it knows and plays by.

112
❖❖❖

I must allow others the benefit of my truths.

We grow up within the security of a family network where truths that will take us through life are ingrained upon us. Hopefully these truths will stand in good stead and allow us to add to them with our own personal experiences.

Not everyone has the luxury of a loving and well-balanced family unit. Instead these individuals will gather to them the truths, as they perceive them to be. Often these truths are built through tough times, but they are still truths as they have proven to be.

Every person has his own catalogue of expertise and experiences gained. Every person is individual and will have their own set of values and beliefs, some of which are rooted so deep, they are rarely considered for their validity and realistic connection with life.

Just for today, become aware of the truths that you share. The words you feel prompted to give might be just the connection needed to guide the receiver back to his next connection of life. Talk your words with kindness, from the bottom line, the truth that is the truth that cannot be swayed. You have your own value to share with the universe and when it is needed someone will always cross your path to use it with.

113
❖❖❖

I am surrounded by light and love. All I need do is connect.

The world is a living ball of energy that has slowed itself enough to form matter. Man is a part of that world. He too is a mixture of living energy and matter. Energy in its fastest form is light. We are all beings of light.

A baby is pure light when it is born. It is brand new and without tarnish. During the course of life, this light can dim and almost appear snuffed out, as troubles, worries, stresses and fears, override our power of freedom and clear thought.

Just for today, become like a child once more. Be open and

receptive to the things this time will bring. Have no fears or preoccupations. Know that you are – and have always been – an important part of the planet you live upon. Reconnect to the source of eternal light and the love that surrounds your every move.

114

❖❖❖

I live each day to the best of my ability.

The day is full of connections and opportunity, each stemming from conscious and unconscious wants and needs that you hold. You transmit out signals every second you are awake. Thoughts turn these connections into reality. They are the driving force behind the power that is you.

Every day is your new page. Write upon it as you will. Let the past be gone and let tomorrow come as it will. Today is where you're at. Today is the place where all possibilities can come into being.

(I am I). I must second this. You do not need to worry. All your needs and desires are known because I know your thoughts. They are your direct line to the universal consciousness that is me. Let go of your fear and let the day flow as it will – as it wants to and as it must. Wherever you are now is simply a fleeting moment in the continuum of space of time, so allow it to exist on its own merit. I must help you to come back to inner peace. (I am I).

Just for today, let go of your fears. Allow the day to simply unfold. Live each moment with the highest intention, to the best of your ability, and at its end look back to see what you have accomplished.

115

❖❖❖

I am a child of the future.

The past has gone. Each generation has the chance to make its mark upon the history timeline. What will you do?

The world is in a state of crisis. Trouble and darkness are everywhere and they will swallow us up if we let them. But will you let them or will you stand tall in the light? Will you be a beacon for others to follow?

The life you live is by your own design. By your own free will and by choice: you are the master and creator of the self you will become. You are not a pawn in a pre-written game, nor are you at the mercy of the life that you are living. You have a strong hold of your destiny in your own hand.

Cause and effect will always play its part and you will live the consequence of your actions, but that is all. You have the ability to step out of the shadows. You alone can channel the steps to a brighter and better version of your life.

Just for today, let the past fall away as well as it is able. Realize the power you have over your own future and take one step at a time as you travel towards it. You alone place your own mark upon history and upon Earth planet itself.

116

❖❖❖

I must be alert for things that need my attention.

Amidst that which we want to do is that which must be done. Just for today, remain open and honest with yourself. Try to complete one or two of the chores that have been waiting silently until you could find the time and inclination to finish them. Take some time to look around at the state of your own affairs and take steps to place them in order. You will not regret it.

117

❖❖❖

I must be willing to bend with and around the flow of life.

The water of a river flows constantly to its source. The river needs no direction or instruction to follow. It simply does what it does.

Man's life should be the same. He too has no set direction, instruction or orders to follow other than those he has placed there himself. Yes, work and commitments intervene, but they are of necessity to his needs. At all other times he is completely his own boss. He has his own choice and free will.

Just for today, allow your life to flow. Follow its call rather than your own. Allow the universe to unfold a little of what is heading your way and go with it. A willow tree will bend and sway in the wind – whether that wind is strong or gentle. You be the same. Bend a little and let go for a while. You may be pleased that you did.

118

❖❖❖

I must be happy in myself.

There is no hard and fast rule to happiness. It is a state of mind available to everyone, yet few can rarely achieve it. In fact, we can spend our whole life chasing its tail without ever catching a glimpse.

The basic nature of man is to achieve, and this can be as varied as the stars in the sky. All that we are, we are, because at some stage, we chose it. We choose all that we do because at that time those choices made us happy. Yet holding onto happiness is another matter. It often seems fleeting at best, and at worst we wonder if we will ever achieve it at all.

Just for today, let go of your hopes, dreams and desires. Exist completely at the place you are now. Allow reality to filter through and stay put for a while. To find happiness you have got to stop chasing your own tail. All that you need is safely within your reach. Take one step at a time and you will get there. Happiness starts with your own peace of mind. Take time to let it filter in.

119

◆◆◆

I must sit in patience and wait.

Man is taught that he must reach out to take all that he needs and all that is his. He is of the impression that to move forward he must force his way through life and its many obstacles. He measures his worth by his accumulation of physical assets and the thoughts that others hold of his place in society. But what does he really think of himself?

The many sides of man can alter and change as many times as he changes his clothes. Who is the real one?

The truth is that he is probably every one of those faces, yet at the same time not any one at all. The real person can be hidden from even the man himself.

Just for today, drop all your facades. Afford others the privilege of seeing the true you. Life is not always a struggle, so allow it to present you with what you need – rather than having to fight for it. The patience you require to do so will be given as soon as you ask. Send your thoughts out to the God mind, to Source – and ask for the patience to wait.

120

❖❖❖

I must be open to receive the light and the truth that lives within me each and every moment.

We are more than the reflection we see in the mirror. This is merely our physical wrapping. It is this physical shell that allows us to experience all that we do in a physical world, a world of matter and decay, a world of harsh realities and the need for improvement within the species that is man.

Through life we get bogged down with worries and stuff. We think that we are alone and that no one cares about anything we try to do. We feel knocked back as we try to move forward and feel stuck to the point of standing still. Yet this is wrong. It is not who we are at all.

The truth is that we are beings of love. We are creation and light in living form. The real you exists deep inside and you know just what that means. The real you tries his or her best to the best, every day. You are feeling bogged down by the fabric that life weaves itself.

Just for today, allow the true you to step out of its shell. Send your thoughts to the God mind, to Source, and ask for your burdens to be lightened and lifted. You need nothing more than what is needed in the present. The universe is waiting to guide you, so open up and let it come to your aid. Every moment you live, allow the best that is possible to manifest through you. You are a work of art that is waiting to be seen for who and what you really are.

121

◆◆◆

I must keep the arena of my mind free from clutter.

The content of our mind is our offering to the universe. It is our connection to the all that exists. It is the version of the self that we usually pay little attention to.

You are the thoughts that you have, the version that exists before you pick and choose. Your thoughts are what you deem yourself to be, how you envision the world and everything in it. Your thoughts are a reflection of the inner you.

Just for today, notice how your actions and words are lead by your thoughts. Notice whether they lead you to truth or to illusion. Whenever possible recycle those you no longer need. Allow your mind to clear itself of clutter every time you call it to question. You are the thoughts that you think, so just for today, choose what you allow to take root.

122

◆◆◆

I must help others find their peace.

You are in charge of your mind. You alone can call it to peace and keep it there.

Peace of mind stems from openness, honesty and truth. When you live each day in the light of these things and always operate from within their boundaries, peace of mind will be yours. When you operate with the best of intention each and every day, when you look for the best in all that you see, truth and peace will be yours.

Just for today, realize that others will follow your lead. The peace that is yours will filter through to them as you communicate and interact by being your natural self. Because you are natural you will always be the same, so others will always know what they will find when they come to seek you out. You will be a constant in a world full of change.

123
❖❖❖

I love my life.

To love one's life is a rare gift. We have highs and we have lows, but to recognize the influence and love of the creator in all things is a rarity that few ever manage.

Because of generations past we can enjoy a bountiful existence where anything and everything is possible. To love one's life does not mean that you must walk daily with stars in your eyes, nor must your life always be a bed of roses. We are human and it is human nature to make mistakes. We live in a physical world of reality, of birth and decay, so this too will leave its mark on the strands of our time.

Instead, to love life is to look back on the events of the day and feel your senses swell with emotion, with love. To see that the good and the not so good have played equally their part and that you have survived, even to smile upon their memory.

Just for today, as you look back in thought, notice the things you have cause to be grateful for. The love that you feel is the gift of creation itself. It is your connection to the Earth you live upon.

124
❖❖❖

All things will happen in their own time.

The life of the world ticks past. It makes its mark in seconds, years, and millennia. The life of every person is but a drop in the time the whole world will exist.

It is man's nature to grow and change. As time passes he must reach out and strive for himself. He must carve out his own niche in this existence.

Being in the right place at the right time seems somewhat haphazard. We suppose we must push, pull and manipulate events to always meet goal expectations, but we are wrong. Yes, we do have free will and yes it is up to us to push the correct sequence of buttons within our affairs, but much that occurs does so with the help and manoeuvring of spirit – the spirit world that links closely with ours. We are not meant to barge blindly from pillar to post, with scarcely a breath. Nothing can happen before it is destined to do so, no matter how much we want or need it to. Nothing can and nothing will happen before all things are set firmly into place, for it to be that way.

Just for today, stop pushing so hard. The universe knows your deepest thoughts. It knows what you want, and even more, what you need for the highest good. Allow necessary links to be put into place so that life will be easier for you. Move with the current of your life rather than constantly swimming against it.

125
❖❖❖

I must be watchful over that which is mine.

That which is yours is not of your physical possession. It is neither material wealth nor matter. It is the essence that is you. It is your lifeline and your soul.

The nature of man is to guard his home, his possessions, his wealth and his hard-gained position, but do we really equate only to this? We are born with nothing and nothing can be taken with us when we leave, so what do we strive so hard to keep?

When our time here is done we take the real gains back home. We take the blue print of all that we are, all that we have known, been, felt and experienced. We take the love we have witnessed and all of its blessings. We take our successes and all our mistakes. We take all that this life has meant in our span, back to the all that is. We take back the link that only we can fulfil.

Just for today, be aware of the person you are striving to be. Take this day as though it were your finest treasure and make the best out of all that you can. You alone can fulfil your place in the history of this space that you occupy. Make this day a day that you will be proud to stand up and have owned.

126

❖❖❖

I must be aware of God's hand in the help that I receive.

Jesus said, 'I am the light and the way. Follow me to the house of my father'.

To be in the light is to live each day for its highest good. We live upon the Earth, the physical body of the universal consciousness. We cannot exist apart from this Earth and the life-sustaining chemicals that it holds. We are part of this Earth plane, just as it is part of us. We are intertwined and interconnected, in all ways.

Nothing exists that the all that is does not know of. Nothing can ever be hidden or removed. There is nowhere to go and no place to hide. How could we hide from God? We live upon his body. Our thoughts are connected to the consciousness that too is his – that is Source – that is Earth.

Just for today, notice the hand of the universe in all that you experience. See it, feel it, know it. How can you not be a part of the whole you live upon? How can you ever be anything else?

127

❖❖❖

I must be open and unbiased in the thoughts that I have.

We aim for specific directions. We hear only that which we need or want at the time. Yet how many of us understand that a whole other universe is operating and integrating with everything we ever do?

Man is a being of energy that houses his physical body. Your body is simply the vehicle that allows you to function as you do upon the Earth. Your body needs oxygen and food to sustain it, but the real you needs only to experience life. The real you thirsts for knowledge, for love, for adventure. You are an explorer in a world of density and matter. You form part of the world that you live upon.

Just for today, allow the explorer in you to come out. Don't hold back, but step forward and allow yourself the luxury of being your own creator. You have this day to use as you will, so what you write upon its page is entirely your own choice. Place your usual expectations high upon the shelf. Be as innocent and as open as a child. Expect nothing, but experience all.

128

❖❖❖

I must remember the happiness of others in my daily doings.

Each day it is necessary to interact with other people. Many do the same things in their life as you. We all have priorities and we all have daily chores, but the variations on this theme are endless. Time and the way we choose to use it is our own individual art.

The happiness of man depends on his ability to enjoy the choices he makes. There is nothing that he does deliberately because he will hate to do it, and nothing is chosen especially to upset his balance and harmony.

Life is a series of interconnecting actions. Happiness relies on our ability to interpret and enjoy them correctly.

Just for today, be aware of what makes you happy. Notice the happiness of others as they interrelate with you. Be aware that, as much as you have feelings and a need to do the things you do, so too do they. The happiness of another is just as important as your own.

129

❖❖❖

I must allow others to come in and out of my life as they will.

The art of acquaintance is a true gift, but too many of us cling too tightly to the people that we connect with. We find it hard to interact and then let go.

People are on their own life's journey, as you are on yours. We can liken this journey to a road on a printed map. Each one will weave and bend as it must, to reach its desired destination. Each road must cross and connect with others along chosen points in its route. There will be pitfalls and deviations but eventually all routes will reach their completion.

Just as your own life is one of these routes, so too are other people's. They have their own courses to follow, but at certain places will run alongside, touch or cross above and below yours. If they were to join your route for too long they would miss their own interconnecting junctures.

Just for today, remember the individuality of other people. Recognize that they might only come into your life for a while. Recognize that although you might really enjoy their company, they cannot stay. A life that touches your own will always enrich it with its presence, but in order to get to where you are going you must uncouple and make your own way.

130

❖ ❖ ❖

I must be happy myself.

When we are happy we are at one with life, even if only every now and again. For a short while we are happy just to be.

Have you ever thought about what makes you happy? Do you laugh out loud for no particular reason at all? Do you sing to yourself or play silly jokes, just because you like to make others laugh?

Happiness is a form of free expression and love. When we are stressed our sense of humour is often the first thing to feel it. The thoughts we have reflect the level we are on. Like attracts like. Laughter always clears the air and is as good for the soul as sunshine.

Just for today, let your hair down and be as innocent as a child in your zest for life. Ask silently that your laughter may come forth and touch all whom you must connect with.

131

❖ ❖ ❖

I must be bold.

Life will flow in the direction it must. There are times when we easily flow along with its course and times when the going gets more difficult. These are the times we must be more vigilant and even more able to let go of the reigns we are tempted to hold onto tighter.

(I am I). These are the times that must be handed over to me for guidance and balance. When the events of the day go nothing as planned, hand things over to me for recycling. Man is more used to digging his heels in deeply when the day runs away with its order. He will shove and pull and shout and stress, just to keep things under control and in the pattern he thinks they should be, but this is where he falls down. When life attempts its own free expression, he pulls it back and squashes it flat. He must learn to be bold, to let it go. There is nothing that I would ever do to harm – only to help. Life cannot always follow his well-planned route. It has a freedom all of its own. (I am I).

Just for today, when people and events refuse to play ball, step back and allow them their space. Send your thoughts silently up and ask for the help to let go. When they have had their moment of freedom, people will cooperate better than before. It takes courage to allow life space of its own.

132
❖❖❖

I must place my problems in the lap of God, of Source...

Problems will always appear, because without them we could never grow forward. They come in all shapes and sizes, fall fast and thick and block our path, but they are also life's indicators that something at this time needs attention. They are signposts that become more demanding when we miss the mark of a gentle nudge.

We are taught that we must stay in complete control of our life. We think that we alone are responsible for the way that life behaves – and in a manner of self, we are. But we are also much more than the self that is visible. We as beings are never alone.

To hold on tightly to a problem as you try to work it through it, simply tells the world of spirit that you want to keep it all to yourself, that you actually want the pain and stress of trying to straighten it out - but the opposite is usually the truth. We hate problems and it is at precisely these times that we should ask for help.

Just for today, when you become blocked by a problem send your thoughts silently and quickly upstairs, to the God mind, to Source. Ask for the problem, situation, issue to be recycled and returned in a manner you can handle easily one step at a time. Ask to be shown the best solution possible at this time. Ask for the help that you need now to show itself. Problems are simply stepping-stones to the place you will be next. In clearing them away you sweep your path to the next clear stretch.

133
❖❖❖

I must be patient with other people.

We are all equal parts of the whole. Race, creed, social standing and colour are ultimately irrelevant. It takes every one of us to complete the life and body that is God, Source.

(I am I). Many grains of sand make up a beach and no grain has

more importance than another. Instead they combine to make the whole thing possible. Man is little different. Ultimately his individuality places him uniquely in his own spot, but it is a combination of all men that make the universal consciousness complete. (I am I).

Each person must live their own truth, their own version of what they deem life to be. Every person will stop and move at their own pace, at their own leisure. They will grow or remain static – again at their own leisure. Two people may see exactly the same thing, but interpret it to be completely different. This is their uniqueness and their strength. Every bit of life is multi-faceted, for that very purpose.

Just for today, be patient with the people who surround you. They are exactly the same as you yet completely different. Recognize that difference because they are only being human after all. We all progress as well as we can in the time that is right for us.

134

❖❖❖

I must be better than I thought I was.

How many times a day do you belittle yourself?

(I am 1). You were created by love – to be loved. You are the essence of me – and I only exist in the love. I can be reached on no other vibration. If I am love and you are a part of my body that you live upon, then how can you imagine that you could ever be anything else? (I am I).

All through your life you unconsciously and consciously search for the love that you feel you are lacking. You search for the love that you think will make you complete. Yet you are already complete – only you do not realize.

How can another person complete you? They too are the same as you. They too unconsciously search for completion. How could they give any part of their self over to you? It is impossible. They can share all the love they have, but even that is not the unconditional love your soul is searching for. They are human and prone to make mistakes. Leaning too heavily on another is a weight that is impossible to carry – for any mortal being.

Just for today, allow yourself to be connected to the universal love at its source. Recognize where you belong. Recognize that the love you have needed was inside you and with you all along. How could it ever not be when you are connected to the source that is God?

135
❖❖❖

I must look at the life pattern that I weave.

We weave the tapestry of our own life, the life that we are choosing to live; but do we look at that pattern as closely as we really aught? Do we look at ourselves from the perspective of how we act and interact with other lives? Would we recognize our own self if we were looking on?

We exist in our own internal world and in this we play the lead part. We try to please others as well as ourselves as we do what we do to our best. But how often do we look at the person we are through the eyes of those we connect with?

When our body dies and we return home the design of our Earthly life is complete. It will be too late to alter one single thing, because all of our time will be spent. If your time were to be over today, would you be pleased with your picture? Would you have woven a life that you would be pleased to have owned, or would you consider it to be somewhat incomplete?

Just for today, be aware of the part that is yours from the point of another.

(I am I). Think of what you are trying to be and why? (I am I).

Are your efforts as true as you think, or do you need to fine-tune them?

136

❖❖❖

I must be living life as I should.

It is necessary to keep our life in balance and order. Too much attention, or not enough in any direction, will keep you in a state of inconsistency.

Each day we have the choice to complete tasks and projects set, or to take on board the distractions that are offered in their place. The choice is up to us.

This day is for you to use as you wish – but at the end of it you must be pleased with your choice. Only you can weigh up your priorities because only you will still have to finish the work that was carried over to tomorrow or the next slot.

Just for today, aim to get past some of the back log of chores that sit quietly in the background but nag when you remember they still wait to be done. The quicker you can move through them, the more free time will be available when you want it.

137
❖❖❖

I must let others have their own opinions.

People are the same in many ways, but they also are completely different in their opinions and needs.

(I am I). Man was created to be my own observer of this Earth that he lives upon. Each person has his or her own unique view of life and its meaning. (I am I).

The world we live in can never be exactly the same for any two people. Their match can come pretty close – but their differences can still be far apart. Even children of the same bloodline from the same family will give a completely different minute-to-minute account of a shared experience.

It is this difference that makes us unique in a life of repetition and moulding. We are all the same, yet hardly the same at all.

(I am I). This is the way it should be. To be all alike would be

pointless, because how could the variety of life exist as it does? (I am I).

Just for today, recognize where you must be the same and fall into line with the surrounding world, but celebrate also in your own uniqueness. You are the only one who can fit the slot that you occupy in the mesh of this Earth. You are the eyes, ears, sense and feeler of your own version of life. Recognize this and allow others the same.

138
❖❖❖

I must recycle my fears instead of holding them in my own self.

The mind is an arena of activity – even in sleep.

(I am I). The mind is the connection that is yours to the universal consciousness that is life, that is me, that is Source. This is the part of you that is eternal. It does not require rest, only stimulation and guidance. (I am I).

The constant movement of the mind is what wears you out when really you have done nothing at all. Energy follows thought and man allows his to run away like water through a sieve. Thoughts churn aimlessly all day long unless we learn to monitor and curb their activity.

Positive thoughts are not too bad, because at least they can uplift you in themselves, but left to multiply at random they can take you on journeys that have little meaning in the time frame you are in.

Negative thoughts are heavier. They will attract like for like until you are completely worn out and fed up. They will attract fear and illusion and will colour the way you interpret your day and the people you are thinking about.

Just for today, still your thoughts as often as you can and bring them back to the task now at hand. Recycle all fear and heaviness and ask that peace and balance remain. Negative energy will stay with you until you make a deliberate and conscious choice to let it go.

139
❖❖❖

I must love myself.

To love oneself is not the same as actually being in love with oneself. The two are completely different.

To 'be' in love with oneself is excessive self-indulgence. The universe centres around you and you think only of its interconnection with your life.

To love your self means the opposite. Again the universe centres around you for it must. In your life you are the central pivot from whence all you are will flow, but there is little opportunity to think of yourself, because you are too busy thinking about others. Your priority in life is to do all that you can for the world that surrounds you, not the big world, but your little corner and connection to it. You live your life by helping and caring. You live a life of service to other people, not because you must, but because it is ingrained in the make up of the being that you are.

Just for today, remember your own needs and necessities too. Look after the being that is you, for without your balance and health the world that you operate from within would suffer. Remember that as you send your thoughts upstairs and ask for help for others, so must you also ask for yourself. This life is run by your own free choice, so, in order to gain what you need, you must first ask for it. If you do not, then the help that you require may not arrive at the appropriate time when you need it.

140

❖❖❖

I must believe in my own efforts.

The universe evolves around each one of us – individually. We are the central pivot from which all that we are will flow.

(I am I). I second this. (I am I).

Evolution dictates that we cannot remain still for too long, for when we do we dry up and stagnate. Nature itself moves in a constant cycle and at every cycle exists a beginning and an end.

For this time in history to move forward many things must reach their ending. Nostradamus himself predicted an end to the world as it was and the new millennium heralded the birth of a new age. Since then mankind has been sorting through much upheaval. Many beliefs, old customs, outdated behaviours and rules have been replaced or thrown by the wayside. We are at a time of new beginnings, both in the outside world and within our own personal lives. Troubles are bringing many things to a head and only when they have been properly addressed will they be put aside, never to return again.

Just for today, take a look at your own life. Are you at the beginning or at the end of a cycle? Are you clearing out your old junk, both materially and in the corners of your mind, or are you planting and sowing seeds that can be harvested at a later date? Have faith in yourself. Wherever you are is the natural progression of choices you have made. There are things that you must pass through before you get to the place you are heading.

141

❖ ❖ ❖

I must believe in my own results.

You are the plant that was grown from the seed that your father and mother once set. You contain both the best and the worst of the characters they were at the time that you were conceived.

The whole of your life has been your training ground. You have worked your way through the input that has had its effect in your world. Everything about you was necessary, to bring you to this point in your journey.

Where you go from here is up to you. The very fact you are reading this book indicates that you are at a turning point. You are looking for fresh input and meaning to the world that surrounds you. Your soul is making connections that you really have always known. You are coming back home to your source.

Just for today, believe in your own latent ability to know exactly where you are going and what it is that you need to take you there. You are a child of the past you have known. You are a product of the future. But most of all, you are everything necessary as a product of this day. Believe in yourself and believe in your results.

(I am I). I do. (I am I).

142

❖❖❖

I must believe my own abilities and worth.

You are the accumulation of all you have ever known, but the place you are heading is not even in sight. This is the beauty of free will and the individual freedom of choice.

Take a dart and throw it at a map. The chance of it landing on the same place twice is almost non existent. Yet so it is also with us. We could travel the whole world over and never come across another version of ourselves: the combination of factors that came together to manifest as the individual who is you, is infinite. You are completely unique in make up, intention, character and intelligence. You are the only one that exists on the face of this Earth.

Many people may appear similar, and some considerably better, we might think, but they too are completely other than the way you perceive them to be. They are also unique.

Just for today, recognize the value in the being that is you. You have spent your whole life becoming the person you are now and will take the remainder to become all that you will. You are unique and you are valuable. You are the only one who can fit in the space that you occupy. So use it well...

143
❖ ❖ ❖

I must let my hand be guided by those who can help.

The hands that are yours are cumbersome and heavy. They are made of physical matter. The hands that try to help and lift you are energy. They are the hands of your angel helpers and guides.

We do not exist alone on the surface of this Earth because we are intertwined. The part of you that is you is really your energy self. It houses the body that gives you a physical existence.

Angels and loved ones who come to help are beings of an even finer energy vibration than we. They come to visit as family and friends do now. When we are in need of assistance they give us support and guidance that they place at our fingertips. All we need do is recognize this when it occurs.

(I am I). I too place the things that you need in your vicinity. I too have been there all through your life, only until now you just

did not realize. How could you, when you were closed to the possibility? You are a living part of me, so how could I turn my back on myself? It is not possible for me to do so. I am living through you. I experience all that you do. When you are sad or in pain, you are imprisoned and closed off to me. You are closed so tightly that I cannot reach you. Only when you ask for help, can I come close enough to feel you once more. You are me, as I am you. We are never separate. (I am I).

Just for today, recycle all blockages brought on by negativity and fear. Ask that truth and peace be your guide. Ask that you can be aware of the help and loving influences that surround you. Remember, this can come forth in any form, from another person to a piece of music, a newspaper article or even a fleeting thought.

(I am I). I will use any means that is available, to reach you when necessary. (I am I).

All you must do is remain open and receptive throughout this day.

144
❖❖❖

I must allow others to co-exist equally in my life.

You are the centre spoke in the wheel of your life, but so too are others in theirs. No one person has ever more importance than another. We are all the same.

The planet that is Earth is the body of God, of Source, and its consciousness lies within, through and all around its own ball of matter. The universal consciousness gives life to the body that is Earth as you provide life to the body that is yours, with your conscious energy.

We all play an equal part in the now of this life, regardless of what has been before and is also yet to come, it is now that matters.

(I am I). Now is the only time that exists in reality. It is now where everything occurs. It is only in the now that changes can be instigated and balance set in its rightful place. All of the future will arise from every now you are in. Be mindful of how you put it into play. (I am I).

Just for today, as you experience your now, remember that others are equally in theirs. They too must put into action the now that their future dictates. No one person is ever more important than the next. The Earth needs us all, and it will take all the focus we possess as a species to guide it safely to its next phase in evolution.

145
❖ ❖ ❖

I must make the most of every day I am given.

This day you are in is a clean fresh page. It is a new start. All that you did yesterday and before, the good and the bad, is over. All that remains in their wake is effect from the cause you put into action.

The life span that you have is precious. It is your gift to the world itself. It is your chance to contribute to the workings of the planet that you live upon. It is your chance 'in time' to put into action the differences you hoped would help mankind become kinder and more loving. It is also your chance to correct some of your own mistakes and to work through a little of the karma that you drag along with you.

Man thinks the world is out of control and that there is little hope for the future, for future generations. He thinks as long as he can survive his little slot, then the rest does not matter, that once he has gone, this place will have nothing to do with him.

(I am I). Does he care so little about the body that is mine? During his time here in the 'now' I moved mountains to help him on his way. I must hope that he will wake up to take better care of the gift he is living, the gift of his life and the difference he will choose to make with it. We are one, man and I. I give my body to him to take care of. Does he not remember? (I am I).

Just for today, take notice of the value of this day. Use it as you would cherish your most prized possession.

(I am I). The day you are in is the beginning of the future. It is a start – not an end. I will give you all the support you need to put it to its highest good. All you need do is realize what you hold in your hand. All you need do is ask. (I am I).

146

❖ ❖ ❖

I must make the best of each moment I am in.

Like a painter uses brush strokes to form his masterpiece, you use minutes and hours for yours. You live your life step by step and choice by choice; all that you are, you did in this manner.

You know the way you have travelled. You know the agony and the pitfalls. You know all your wrong decisions and you know your best ones as well.

The future is yet unwritten, even though its general direction might be known. Before you get there you will make a billion decisions along the way. You might arrive at where you think your goal posts lie only to realize that you do not want to be there after all; and again you will re-choose and take another path to another destination of your own free will: because you can; because that prerogative was given to you as your birthright.

Just for today, be aware of the life you are creating. Will it be your masterpiece or your regret? Take this moment in 'time' that is offered and place things how know they should be. Take a moment to repair any damage and instead plant the seeds that you would rather reap. Remember, you are already blessed by the fact that you are now beginning to realize the importance of the time you have left. Others might not yet be so fortunate.

147

❖ ❖ ❖

I must allow thoughts to filter through as they will and then I must choose to let them go.

Until the time you wake up to the life that you choose for yourself, you operate on automatic pilot with a mind that is more used to free reign. The mind is out of control until you pull it back with your reigns. You have charge over it, not it over you.

Thoughts operate on a link system. One will always trigger the next until you decide to change the subject or become jolted back to reality itself. The mind needs food and stimulation, and this it will take from wherever it can if not consciously forthcoming from you.

Information covers many subjects. It is also the cause of the turmoil that exists both within and without the human form. Information bombards our senses from morning to night, but how often do we register its relevance to ourselves or to the life that we connect to? How often do we allow mindless rubbish to overtake rational thought and our own internal affairs?

Just for today, be aware of what you allow your attention to tune into. Remember that escapism is fine as long as you recognize your reality. Your mind is yours to take by the reigns, and you must.

148

❖❖❖

I must make myself busy when I should be.

Time is precious. It is one thing to know it, but completely another to recognize and live this as truth.

We all know what we aim to achieve in any one day. We know our ideal and we also know the minimum, yet how easy it is to let it all slip away.

Excuses and interruptions will always be plenty. Man must work to keep himself on track. He alone must carry the load that drags at his heels until it's dealt with. He is as responsible for his shortcomings as he is for his talents.

Just for today, recognize the things that you put off – probably once again – until another day. When you under achieve, you simply place the burden you should now have dealt with again in your path, and so deliver it into your future. The present time, you have been wasting.

149

❖❖❖

I must make myself my timekeeper.

The clock can monitor the transition of time but only man can harness it and put it to use.

(I am I). The passage of time is not relevant, but the way man

chooses to spend it is. He is totally responsible for the life that he will live or squander. This is the law that is written in spirit. This is the rule of time. (I am I).

Just for today, be aware of the time that is yours. Be wise in the way you use it and be careful to not let it go to waste.

150

❖❖❖

I must listen to my better judgement at all times.

We are pulled all over the place by the many voices that talk in our head. Some are loud and demand that we listen, whilst others are heard and then thrown away. Then there are those that reoccur. They wait in the corner for quieter moments until we hear and take them on board.

Your ego is very often the most deafening noise that speaks in your head. It is this that works the buttons you normally respond with, in your daily interaction to life. It is this that measures your own self worth and how you then proceed. The Ego will rule over all that you are, until you recognize that it lives to put obstructions in your life.

Just for today, send your thoughts quietly upstairs. Ask that your ego may be gone. Ask for peace and light to fill its place and for reality to now be your guide. Ask for illusion to be lifted until you know the truth that is yours.

151

❖ ❖ ❖

I must listen to the voice of truth and love and reason.

(I am I) How can you listen but not even hear? Man is so locked in his own personal thought waves that, unless he learns to hear the sounds that are spoken, he will stay locked in the darkness forever. (I am I)

The world is in turmoil, because of a lack of understanding, communication and respect. Even people of one family find it hard to get along, and as we look to the wider world we can see evidence of this en mass, every day.
The harder we fight to communicate, the tougher the problems become, yet there in itself is a key. We should not fight – for any reason. Fighting to be heard is simply fighting for the same space – the same slot in time.

(I am I) To fight is to lose and to lose means there is no win. To fight for the same space means that you simply cancel each other out. You negate one another. All parties feel unheard and rejected. I am the only way forward. Give to me all that you don't want, all that you don't need. Ask for my help and I will recycle and correct the whole situation. Send me your turmoil and I will replace it with peace and understanding. (I am I)

Just for today, when you think you are misunderstood or you misunderstand the words and deeds of another, sit yourself down and be still. Allow your mind to be tranquil as you ask with your thoughts for truth to shine through. Let the matter rest until it comes back to you with love and with reason attached. There are always at least two sides to any story and possibly at times even more. The light of the creator, of Source, will always show through when you let it.

152

❖❖❖

I must look to God, to Source, to help me through the times when I need help.

Your father and mother gave you life. They grew the body that you live in now. They shared with you the best and the worst they had to offer – but more than that, they are people. People who had hopes and dreams like yourself. People with fears and feelings and shortcomings of their own.

The life that you live, you do so in spite of all of your sufferings. You do so in spite of your better judgement and your own higher learning. You are a work in progress that will not be complete until your last breath is drawn, but even then you will still grow forward in the life that is you.

(I am 1) I have left man always the run of free will. Any mistake he will make will simply be that – his mistake. Would a loving parent turn his back on his child when he makes a lack of judgement, when he takes a wrong path until he knows better? No they would not and neither will I. I have vowed to be with you throughout, till the end. You are a breathing and living expression of myself, so how could I turn my back on me? You are me, but you do not remember it yet. You stumble and err, because at this time you believe you are alone and no one, but a close few will know what you do. You think you can stumble through life and then it all will be done. The truth can never be further than the picture you think it to be. I am always only one

thought away. (I am I)

Just for today, help yourself by asking for help, in any way at all that you need it. This is your life and there is no rehearsal. You are the one in control of your 'now'. You are the only one who can make that connection to the help that waits by your side.

(I am I) The thoughts that you send out to me are always received. I will use any means that your intelligence can grasp to reach you in return. You will never be alone when you look for the love that waits in the truth of the moment. I am not a fairy tale, but real, and when you learn to reach out, you will find the proof that you require – for I will give it. (I am I)

153

❖❖❖

I must be careful to recycle my fears at all times.

The power of thought and action far exceedes anything that many can understand at this time. The power of energy as the by-product of thought and action is even greater on this physical plain of matter, where thought makes matter, and action renders it stone.

The balance of all that exists is critical, now more than ever.

(I am I) The balance of this Earth plane rests in the lap of man. It is only he, with his conscious thought, that can place order where chaos is rampant. Man must make the first moves by his own example and slowly it will filter out towards the larger world. (I am I)

Negative energy is all-consuming. Fear, anger, jealousy, guilt, stress, worry and sadness are all negativity based. They pull you down until you say and do all sorts of things that otherwise you would not. Left to fester, negative emotions will keep you in a state of illusion and depression until life is too heavy and hard to bear.

(I am I) This is a trouble of man today. This is the weight he will carry inside, until he learns not to anymore. This is where I help him. I will hear his thoughts when his heart calls out for aid. The smallest plea made in sincerity and love will always be carried to those who wait there for him, always. He is not alone, but part of a team, the majority of whom are connected through parentage, but can only help when asked. (I am I)

Just for today, recognize the value of yourself and your life, because everyday is important, it must be lived to its fullest potential. Recycle all negative feelings and emotions as soon as they arise. Ask silently that the truth and light and love of your birthright take you forward for your highest good.

(I am I. You create your reality with the thoughts and choices you make. If you are unhappy, find out where, find out why, and ask for help to re-choose. (I am I)

154

❖❖❖

I must learn to wait.

The world took time to evolve and mature the way it is today. Nature has itself a definite cycle of time to uphold, to retain balance and health and order. Man has lost his own state of balance because he has lost his patience. He will not wait for the law of cause and effect to take hold.

To wait is not always easy. Man lives at a fast pace where hours and days cost money. He chomps at the bit like a racehorse, to be first off the mark and first at the goal; but first is not always best.

Nothing can be born and nothing will bear fruit until the time that it should do so. At an unseen level many influences work hard to put things into place for the time they are needed. When we race ahead of ourselves with impatience, we often get to the mark too soon. The help that was destined and needed for completion has now gone out of sync. Man has tried to fast-forward his time.

Just for today, when it is necessary to wait, then do so. Wait with the confidence of knowing that all things will be as they should be. What is to be yours will be so, and what you lose was never yours to be had in the first place. Send your thoughts up to the universal mind and ask that patience be yours. Ask for all things to be put into place for the highest outcome for your highest good.

155
❖ ❖ ❖

I must not hurry through the time that has been allotted to my life.

The expanse of a life is but a drop in the ocean of time.

(I am I) Man will live many times, but each life will gain more importance than the last. As the journey of his soul progresses, it must realize the importance of its time here on Earth. (I am I)

Man has chosen to undertake the journey of this life. The importance of that journey may be known as he travels along, or it may not become known before he returns home to spirit. Whenever and wherever he chooses to wake is his own affair, but it is clear that he will not easily do so, until his allotted time.

All that man must experience, he will do so. He will live by his choices alone and will bear the cost of his experience. He will follow his free will and still may not be completely happy. His world may be full with treasure and respect, but still he may not feel whole. Until he discovers universal law, he will always think something is missing. He will be chasing his illusion, not his reality.

Man is completely interconnected to the whole that is. Nothing can ever be hidden because all action has its equal effect along the grid of consciousness of which he is part. He is the keeper of the life that is his to occupy, and because it is individual he is uniquely qualified to fulfil this post.

Just for today, recognize the gift that is your life. Ask God, Source, to slow down your perception of time until you can savour every moment you are in. Enjoy the sensations, the love and the friendship of all life's experience. Have the most you can get from this day and love it for all of its worth.

156

◆ ◆ ◆

I must let others play the part that they must in my life.

Your life is but a tiny fragment in the picture of this day.

(I am I) The importance of each is immense, because without it, that picture could not be complete. (I am I)

Life is a work in motion. To sustain itself it must never stand still or it will be replaced with another vibration. Life must flow.

(I am I) Life is never still, because without movement, it would not be alive. (I am I)

Man forms his part of this movement. He is responsible for the energy he creates and transmits. He manoeuvres it from place to place until it integrates with the energy of others.

The Earth is alive. It's heaving mass of energy and light sustains us as we sustain it. Man is also a mixture of energy and light, and as so we form our part in this Earth. We are responsible for vibrations that flow through us, for the quality of energy we exchange with others, and they are responsible for theirs.

Just for today, allow other people to come and go as they must. Each person has his own role to play as his part in the life of the planet. He must make his connections, as you must surely make yours.

157

❖ ❖ ❖

I must keep my own thoughts open and uncluttered.

Thought waves are the signals that attract like to like. Thought makes a connection wherever it can. Thought is an energy pulse capable of life.

Imagine your mind to be an empty room, in a beautiful building in a beautiful setting. Wealth and abundance exist all around, but still the room is an empty room. It is incapable of knowing just what it is and how lucky to be part of its whole. The room needs dressing and integrating to have any meaning at all.

The mind of man is the same. How can it know what it is without aid and direction? The mind is as a child that needs nurture and care and knowledge. Given these correctly, it is capable of more than we know, but left to itself like a child without guidance, it cannot work as it should.

The mind needs its boundaries and guide lines to help it know right from left, high from low, hot from cold... Piece by piece it makes its own map of experience and learns to accept, adapt and reject things accordingly.

Just for today, keep your mind centred and focused on reality, on the now of your life. Ask silently that all clutter be lifted and that truth and light remain in its place. Be aware that generated thoughts are responsible for creating the life that you choose. They also are your offering to the energy grid of the planet.

158

❖❖❖

I must keep my life free of fear.

Fear – a small word in itself, but probably one of the most troublesome. It comes in many unsuspecting guises that are so normal in daily life that we don't even realize they are there.

Like attracts like, and fear, a negative emotion, will linger all day and get worse. The anger of others can cause fear in us. Stress rubs off and sticks to us. Worry, jealousy and apprehension are all by-products of fear. Trouble of any kind is fear cloaked in a different guise. What you must do is realize this, and learn how to let go.

Fear is a heavy emotion. It is usually felt or carried in the top of the stomach, the chest, the neck or back, either in the lumbar region or across the shoulders. It can feel like a knot, a lump or an ache, but by learning to recognize its onset, you have the choice of whether or not to accept and carry it. You can add to it with the thoughts that you generate, or you can choose to release it and let it go.

Learning to recognize your body's own signals will be a huge leap in keeping you clear. Until now your mind has churned out thoughts of its own accord, but you are changing the rules. With practice you will alter the pattern it lives by.

Just for today, recognize your thoughts and recognize the feelings you have in your body. Any form of fear is hampering. It is unnecessary in the day you are in, so ask for it to be lifted. Ask that illusion be recycled and that truth, love and balance remain. The peace that your mind needs to focus as it should is up to you to obtain. Fear is its decoy.

159
❖❖❖

I must keep my mind at peace in order that the truth can filter through.

Fear is a blockage to the mind and your higher self. To remain at peace is to remain open, and to be open to the experiences of life is the highest goal of being free.

(I am I) I made man to take life as it flows, to take the moment he is in, to experience its wonder. I made man in the image he is, to be able to live life as he does. (I am I)

To experience life as it arrives we must be open and unhampered by boundary and expectation. To experience life in the full is to have no expectation at all. Each day and each moment is individual. It may be similar to others you have had, but this day is its own – for its own merit.

To retain an open mind is the highest goal of a guru. It is the ultimate gift to the self and to the universal consciousness. To keep an open mind despite any turmoil around you will allow love and truth to be with you – always. You are never alone – yet how can you know that when you remain on the treadmill of chaos? Allow the advice and help that is needed to filter through to your thoughts.

Just for today, let peace in your mind be the order of the day. Focus on nothing but the task at hand. When your thoughts drift off, gently bring them back. Take notice of where they have been and gently let them go. Allow any truths to come to you. Let the day unfold as it will and allow yourself to let it.

160

❖❖❖

I am an open channel for light and for love.

You are a being of light. The colours within your spectrum are too glorious to describe. In fact, there is nothing within our language that could adequately portray the splendour of the true human species.

(I am I) Pure, white, brilliant light is the light from which you came. White light is how you would describe me – if indeed your eyes could behold such a light. Man is part of who I am. He is part of the body, my body that he lives upon; part of my body is a permanent part of him. The two can never be separate; the two are part of one another. The purest, whitest, brightest light is a mirage of spectacular colour. The life that is you is also a mirage of colour. Know that this is true and begin to know the full beauty of the being you are. (I am I)

Just for today, recognise that the truth of your life will always be visible, not on this Earth plain, but in your blue print, the energy being that is you. You are a channel for all that is good, or all that is not, to flow through you. You choose to connect with the higher consciousness of this Earth, or to the negative depths. You are a being that was made from love, and you are capable of being love in its truest form. The choice has always been yours.

161

❖ ❖ ❖

I ask that I may see not with my eyes and my feelings but with the truth that exists within my very being.

Each person is endowed with a sound sense of right and wrong. This is accumulated over time and becomes finely tuned as life progresses. The majority will live accordingly. Yet how often do we feel that these truths run contrary to our beliefs? How often do we listen to our gut instincts, and how often do we wish that we had?

The truth of man will change and grow according to culture and belief, and according to the progression of his soul. His truths rely also on being told the truth in the first place. Yet an even deeper truth is part of us all.

Man is connected to the Earth and the Earth has born witness to all that ever was. It is a living, breathing intelligence to which we all belong. How could we believe that we know all the answers? We have only to look within our own lifeline to see that clearly we don't. The Earth and Man's connection will grow far beyond anything we could begin to imagine now.

Just for today, see past what your eyes and ears and feelings are telling you. None of these senses are as reliable as you believe. Allow yourself to calm down and ask for the real truth to show itself. Ask and you will be given. That is your heritage.

162

◆◆◆

I ask that I may hear not with my ears, but with the part of me that is connected to the light of the world.

The ears do not always serve man as well as they might. What we think we hear and the words being said are often two different things. We hear with the thoughts and opinions of others as well as our own. Feelings and mood swings will also play their part.

The vocabulary of man is very limiting. Words frequently fall short of the meanings we aim to portray. Feelings and love are too large to be explained, while hate and malice fall fast from the lips. Man must open his mind. This is the only way forward. He must lose all illusion and left over emotion. He must realise that this is a new day, another page that waits for his input. The rules of yesterday no longer apply. Pain and hurt must be laid aside until he is able to communicate directly from the heart.

We all need the same basic things from this life – to love, to be loved and to fit. Misconnection stems from misunderstanding and misunderstanding stems from the fear of not being heard or felt or known.

Just for today, let this day be understood. Allow others to speak their words without inner conflict from you. Allow yourself to convey your own truth and know it will be understood. Ask silently that you may be given the words you need and that the highest good for all can be met.

163

❖❖❖

I ask that I may be the sum total of all that I am destined to be.

Life is long, yet it is incredibly short, and we shorten it further as we wish it away and keep our thoughts running on automatic pilot. We live in a box and forget that life is here to be lived.

The place you are at in your life is probably just another stepping stone. It will lead you to your future as your past has led you to now. You are not destined to stand still and be bogged down. You are not meant to plod through each day to keep all things the same.

To remain the same too long is to stagnate. Open a window and let some new air come in.

Just for today, understand that the universe is working with you – for you and through you. Allow yourself to be swept along and enjoy the ride. The tracks of your life run deep, and to make any change may feel strange for a time – but don't stop. You are simply letting go of the patterns you no longer need. Like a pair of old shoes with holes, you would keep wearing them still if you could, but life can be like that too. All you have ever been, you were meant to be, but all you will ever become is calling, so allow life some space to manoeuvre.

164

❖❖❖

I must place my trust in a loving, caring God.

The day you are in is yours to live, but it is also the beginning of your future.

We clearly know what needs to be done, we know where we have been and we aim loosely for the future, but we have little idea what will be around the next corner; and it is this that will determine our path.

Nothing is ever completely rock solid because all things are subject to change. The very nature of life is to change, or it would not be alive at all.

To follow a map on a predestined route is easy, because the beginning and the end are certain. The route you can choose, because always you will reach your designation; but life is nothing like that. We have little idea of where we'll end up or what the future holds in store. We make it up as we progress.

Nothing is written to follow and few goals are formed out of stone. We are open-ended until the end, and that is the nature of true creation. We create our own life and its destiny with the invisible laws of cause and effect.

Just for today, lay all forging ahead to one side. Your hopes and desires have already been recognized by those who can put them into action. There's no need to pull strings or barge through this time. Step back and get focused on the now. Do all that you must do and allow life to unfold as it will. It will be in your interest to do so.

165

❖ ❖ ❖

I must be patient to allow life to flow as it should.

Your life is important and to you it is everything, but in the scale of the whole it plays just one small part.

Man is the central pivot in the universe that he knows. All that he is will start first with him, and this is the way it must be. The whole of this Earth is made up the same way with each part at the centre of its stage.

When we loose our inner balance, we affect life like a top spinning out of control. We send signals and turbulence to everyone around. We are in fact looking to fit, but because we don't know where that fitting is, we tumble about until we do. The niche that we fill will feel fine for a time but it is not always the answer to the end.

(I am I) I have also to search through life. This is the nature of growth. Man cannot be who he was destined to be until he is completely sure of the person he is not. After major upheaval,I how can he connect immediately with his true place in life? Trauma leaves man troubled and unsure. All that he clung to is gone. The person he was is now changed. How can he connect immediately to the place he will later end up? The first connections he makes will be to repair and make himself better, and only when he is whole again can he take up his future once more. (I am I)

Just for today, recognize exactly where you are on your path. Are you safely secure in your happy ever after or do you feel there's still further to go? Are you on a sidetrack waiting to take the next step or are you on your steppingstone? Ask your higher self to lead you to where you must be. Ask for negative forces to be lifted now and to place peace and love in its wake. Allow life to flow a little and you may be pleased that you did.

166

❖❖❖

I must have faith that the future will be as it should be.

The world of matter is heavy and dense, but its weight lies not in these places. The weight that ties man down is the weight of his spirit — the burden in his soul.

A baby born to Earth is new and light. It is a new spirit without any baggage.

(I am I) A new spirit born to partake of this world; a new explorer; a creator – just like myself. (I am I)

When this spirit grows, it will draw upon the lessons it has learnt while on the Earth plain. It will look to its boundaries and limitations to know itself and its talents. Yet the truth of its abilities go far beyond the boundaries of matter. The truth lies in man's soul.

(I am I) The soul of man is the part that is me. It is the blue print of the being he is, not just now at this time, but for all the time he has lived, as far back as that might be. (I am I)

His blue print is himself in his truest form. It is here that his individuality lies.

(I am I) It is here that his hopes, dreams and aspirations exist. It is here that his talents can be accessed, and the help that is ordained and obtained. It is here that he is never alone, because he is part of a chain, of a team. He is part of the universal consciousness, so it is here that all can be accessed. (I am I)

Just for today, realize the truth of your identity. Allow Earthly limitations to fall away and be that being of light. The life you are living is but a shadow of the life that is yours. Use this day in honour of the possibilities that exist, as part of the path that is yours.

167
❖❖❖

I must trust myself to choose the correct path.

The life you have lived, you have done so by choice. You have decided what to do along the way. You have aimed for your goal and headed that way as opportunity and expertise presented themselves. All that you are is by your own creation, nurtured by peers and by friends, but all that you know and all you are now are a long way from the person you could be.

No limitations exist on this Earth to prevent your evolution. You are bound only by your thoughts and your deeds. You have commitments and loved ones, but that is a part of life. It is part of belonging and being. Your thinking and the barriers you erect bind you instead. You are bound by your belief that the life you commit to is the end of the line. It is not.

(I am I) The person that you are is the person you 'think' yourself to be, but really you have no limitation. You are limited only by your soul's progression within this Earth life. You are limited only by your thoughts, intentions, deeds and knowledge. Planted inside is the ability to break free of those binds – to evolve as a butterfly comes from a grub. The knowledge you have gained is but a drop in the ocean of understanding that is available to all. You are part of the universal consciousness. You are part of creation itself. (I am I)

Just for today, take a look at your life; it is built by you, on the understanding that you are matter alone. You must have your love, your family, home and job. You must have the necessities that keep all these going; but other than that you are free. Your commitments are part of the life you are living, and these too you will address one by one; but other than that begin your search. Look for the truth that surrounds you. Look but don't stress, because when you are ready, the knowledge you require will start to appear. You are where you are supposed to be, but now it is time for some growth.

168

❖❖❖

I must look after myself when I need to.

Your body is the vehicle that enables you to live this experience. It is not a temple but it does need care and consideration. It does not require unending attention but it does need to be properly looked after.

You are a living mechanism and as such are subject to the laws of decay; but apart from that you will live a full and healthy life. Illness comes when the body breaks down, as a machine may have weak spots too. But you are not just your body. You are more and it is this more that can replenish what is lacking. It is this more that can protect you through life.

Illness comes not only from weakness of tissue, but from energy blockages too. Man is a channel for Earth's energy to pulse through. Without proper care and attention, his channel will become blocked, and where there is blockage there is a problem.

(I am I) Man operates through his body, but a blockage will cut him off from his source. It will transform the frequency of his energy into a denser matter, and over time he becomes ill. (I am I)

Illness over time causes problems in the body, and problems in the body will hamper man's ability to experience the life of his choice. He is caught in a cycle that needs to be broken, and for this he must look to his self.

Just for today, look to see where your blockages are, either in your body or the life that surrounds you. All you will find is but a reflection of discord that is blocking the being that is you. If you are ill, see a doctor. If you know that you are well, but yet still feel ill, then the problem lies deeper than skin. It is time for you to research the reasons you feel as you do. An inner feeling of disharmony needs recycling. Send your thoughts quietly up to the help that is there and ask for all you might need to reveal itself. Ask that your burden be lifted and that peace and love and health be yours now.

169

❖ ❖ ❖

I must be understanding when others around me go a little wobbly.

The best-laid plans will sometimes go amiss, because we cannot anticipate outside interference.

We all know that mistakes can happen, and when they do, they drop with a clang.

(I am I) Man must remember that he is human and therefore prone to error. (I am I)

Yet sometimes we forget that others too can fall down. Mistakes happen as a part of life. Anger also is a part of life but in the required dose and at the appropriate time.

The things that fall out of sync usually do so because of a reason. Find the reason and you find the problem.

Just for today, be understanding when others are having a bad day. They don't need you to battle with too. Instead send out your thoughts and ask for some help. Ask that their burdens be lifted and that help may come to their aid. The thoughts you send out will be more of a blessing than you know.

170

❖❖❖

I must speak my highest truth at all times.

Each person has his own truth. It is his view of his world as he believes it to be.

(I am I) The truth is always the bottom line, free of fancy and free of illusion. (I am I)

To communicate, we connect with other people and those then connect with others still. This forms part of the universal grid. All truths must be shared at the appropriate time to fill in the gaps that are waiting. Information moves from point to point at exactly the time it is needed. When things run well, everyone is fulfilled; but when a hitch arises, the flow breaks down. Substitute the word information with energy and you have an idea of the importance of communication. Man moves energy around the planet, from him, through him and to him.

To speak your truth means that you give a clear and constant signal, always. You provide a good clear picture for others to connect to. When people lie, they give false information, and again the system breaks down. To say nothing at all is still just as bad, because you miss the cue that was yours. Others will then have to work harder to continue without that specific link. You can begin now to see how connections are made and the importance of each part you play.

Just for today, make all that you say your highest truth. Speak nothing else.

171

❖ ❖ ❖

I must expect the best when I give the best.

The law of cause and effect runs completely through all of this life. The Earth was formed by it. Man was born of it and all things stem from it. Nothing will ever slip past it, because all things are written in the code of the Earth.

Man has a record of all that he is. The Earth has its own record too. Like attracts like as the law says it must, and all that we do we gain back.

Every day is a new day and a chance to do things better. When we aim for the higher good we make better decisions and work towards peace. We give the best we have to offer – always.

Just for today, operate from your highest intention. Let peace, love and truth be your goal.

(I am I) When you operate from within the light you work in sync with the law. What you give out you will always get back and what you will reap you must share. (I am I)

We are all equal parts of the whole.

172

❖ ❖ ❖

I must be prepared to ask for what I need when it's not forthcoming in the manner that it should.

All people are alike, yet we all are completely different. That is the paradox that is man.

(I am I) The difference is what gives you your edge. Your individuality is what makes you you. (I am I)

A common mistake is to believe that others can know what you need. How can they when they exist outside of your being? How can they know what you will expect from any given day and situation? They must take care of the things that they need themselves, so when you feel let down or ignored, tell someone first what you need.

The needs of man vary as often as the weather. What is fine on this day may not be on another. Emotions, stress, requirements change. The needs of individuals alter along with the pressures of life.

Just for today, understand that others might not know what you are thinking. Only you can feel your emotions and feelings. You know what you need and the time that you need it, so let others in on that too. Don't expect – ask. Don't get lonely – ask. Send your thoughts upstairs to the God mind and ask that all your needs be met.

173

❖❖❖

I must allow mistakes to be rectified.

Mistakes. What is the true definition?

Mistakes are deeds done in error, either wilfully or not. Mistakes are the problem of everyone. We all make them. They are done both in the name of love and of hate. No one is immune. This is the problem we must carry.

Knowledge is to broaden ones mind, and as we do we see a larger and clearer picture of the world. Belief is another thing. The belief of a man can be ingrained from childhood but it is not always the product of truth. The belief of a man means that he just trusts the things he's been told. If he is fed illusion, he will believe it to be true. If he is led by one, or by many, who are false, then he too will become the same.

Knowledge must cover all truths. It must be able to withstand question and scrutiny. It must open the door for further discussion, for further research and an even deeper probing. Knowledge is open to all and when it withstands these tests and survives, it is true.

Mistakes happen through a lack of something, perhaps understanding or attention, perhaps too much haste or not enough. Mistakes are the product of man.

Just for today, when someone makes a mistake, recognize it. Take the trouble to understand its cause and allow it then to be rectified.

174

❖ ❖ ❖

I must stop back tracking on the things that I do.

Have the trust in yourself that you deserve. You must stop questioning your every move. You know the difference between right and wrong. You do the jobs well that you do. If you don't trust your own judgement and ability, then how can you expect others to trust in you?

An air of uncertainty has a negative vibe. The people that surround you will feel it. Uncertainty can only breed more uncertainty, because how could it ever be right? To be uncertain means failure to commit, and non-committal means you cannot be sure. To be unsure means you don't know the answer, until you break the cycle you are in.

To back track means that you've missed something, that you are again unsure of yourself. Can you see how you make things worse for yourself? Can you see why you need to be sure?

Just for today, be sure of everything you do. Take the trouble to do things properly, correctly and positively. When everything you do is positively done, how can you ever be unsure?

175

❖ ❖ ❖

I must be free to go forward without the pain and fear that keeps me anchored in my past.

The past has past. It will not be anymore. All that happened there is also past. Today is a brand new day.

No life will ever be free of issue, pain or torment. People will always do what they ought not to, because they believe that they can. They believe that no one will know. They think – or don't think, and that is the problem. The pain that is suffered because of the past must be lifted. The past cannot reach you any more.

The law of cause and effect only comes into play once the cause has been activated. The effect is the product of the cause. Allow your effect to fall away now.

You have the rest of your life to live. It can be all that you dream it to be. You hold the key and you have free rein. You must write your own rules.

Just for today, ask that you can move beyond the pains of the past. Ask that your fear be removed and healing put into its place. All who inflict hurt and pain in another must be brought to account for their action.

(I am I) The love that you need is within. Take a moment to reach in and find it. I will help you when you ask it of me. 1 will replace fear with peace and love. (I am I)

You make the choice of whether this day will be love, or under the control of your past.

176
❖❖❖

I must believe the impossible.

To walk on the moon was impossible. To sail around the world was impossible. To heal with only your hands was impossible. To fly like a bird was impossible. To believe in God's love – impossible.

The folly of man is to believe in limitations; yet no man and no thing hold or bind him. All that he dreams is quite within reach.

(I am I) Man has the power to supersede mine. He has the free rein of his life. I only live through him. I can only know the real meaning of physical life through his conscious action and thought. (I am I)

Just for today, believe in the seemingly impossible, for in reality there is no such thing. Man holds the possible in his very grasp. Nothing will stand in his way.

177

❖ ❖ ❖

I must be able to trust myself.

Who can trust you despite all the things you know you have done?

(I am I) I can. (I am I)

There is no love upon the face of this Earth that can match the unconditional love that surrounds you from God. This is not fairy tale, but fact.

The reason that man searches through life to feel loved and to belong is that he thought he was disconnected from the whole. He thought he was on his own and that all love he obtained was only to be his for a price. And it is this price that keeps him locked in the fear, away from the very thing he is needing. It is this price that makes him hide the parts of himself that he believes unworthy, like a black sheep or skeletons in the closet. He must understand that he is wrong. He is surrounded by the love that he cannot ever disconnect from. He is a child of God. He is God's son.

Because you are who you are you cannot hide, but then why should you? You are not being judged, because you do that for yourself. You are not being moulded, pushed, blamed or punished. You are simply being asked to wake up to the truth; to live your life to its highest possible outcome and to enjoy every experience that this life and Earth planet have to offer.

Just for today, let go of your armour. Learn to trust in yourself. You could not know the importance of life until the time that you did. Trust that you will not waste your days. Allow yourself to be you, but remove your unwanted rubbish.

178
❖❖❖

I must immerse my emotions in peace at all times.

The emotions that are yours are yours to control. Any thoughts that are generated should be done in a balanced way, for only then can you remain open, honest and unbiased.

People will push all your buttons. They might not know or even care that they do. Life will present you will all that it does, for no other reason than it must. To avoid life is to stagnate, and when that becomes reality you have to have a kick-start. Life will do all it can to get you rolling once more. Life is your friend – never your foe, and if you think it is, then you have got to grow.

Life is both positive and negative. It needs light and dark for its balance. The two sides of life will bring you your own inner balance as you learn not to overreact. When you have turmoil, remain calm and find your way through it. When you are happy, don't get overexcited. Balance will add to the experience. Have a good time, but don't go over the top.

Just for today, allow your inner state of balance to guide you. In this mode you will feel the slightest pull from either direction. You will be more alert than you have ever been and therefore more in tune with your soul. When you feel fluctuation arising, send your thoughts up to the God mind, to Source, and ask to be bought back to peace. Ask that all excess energy and emotion be harvested and placed where they are needed the most; to better someone else in their day.

179

❖❖❖

I must allow God, Source, to lead me forward.

We think we have control of our life, and indeed we do, but we don't always know what is best for us at any given moment.

Freedom of choice and decision are ours. We decide our next move – always. From childhood we learn to follow our instincts and to follow the lead, but sometimes we are not very sure. When there is more than one route to choose from we can dither and worry and fret. We talk to friends to give us a hint, but they sometimes don't understand.

When you don't know the direction to go, don't worry. Sit back, sit tight and do nothing. When you are back at a place you know you have been before, don't worry. You must have missed the point the first time around. When you are pushed hard to make your decision, but it feels too much of a rush, stop and wait until you know exactly what you must do – without doubt.

Just for today, understand that you are not on your own. Someone else is watching over you and leading you forward. They know all you have been through and all you must face. Send your thoughts to the universal consciousness – to God. Ask that all your dilemmas be lifted and that you might clearly know which choice to take. Ask for peace and love to be the guide of your higher self for your highest good.

180

❖❖❖

I must keep my words brief and to the point.

When we get asked our opinion, the opportunity to communicate might be only brief. This is the time we have their attention. This is the time that the response we give matters most.

It is human nature to be opinionated, for we all carry a version of the truth. And what is the truth, but to share, especially when it is called for? Words can be long and they can be very colourful. They can even be extremely unhelpful.

Just for today, limit the words that you choose. To keep hold of someone's interest; keep things real and to the point. Don't switch tracks and speak of your own experience and fancy, just be open and honest and kind. When you don't know what to say, send your thoughts up for help and guidance, ask that the words needed now might be given.

181

❖❖❖

I must keep love in my heart at all costs.

(I am I) I ask my children to reconnect with me. I can reach them nowhere but in the love. I can help them nowhere but in the love. (I am I)

To be in fear is to be closed off from life. It is to operate alone, and to fight through your life. Yet this is not the only way to exist.

When man is open he has love in his heart. He is able to swim alongside the currents of life, so that there he will feel least resistance. He is able to think on a positive note and therefore will attract the better outcome. He is tougher because he is surrounded by truth, and this in turn means more positive energy. Of course there will be times that he feels knocked back, but in the love zone he is better able to recover. He will not feel the full force of the negative blow.

Just for today, ask that love may be your shield, your cloak and your guiding light. Ask that all else may fall away. Ask the light to stay with you – always and trust in your heart that it is there, that you have been heard and that now you will be safe.

182

❖❖❖

I must never forget the extent of my spiritual heritage.

All through life man craves acceptance. He works hard to achieve his talents, but at the bottom line he needs to be understood for the person he really is. He needs recognition for his sense of self-worth.

War, turmoil, physical strife and unrest will all leave their mark on the personality itself, and man is taught at an early age that he must push past and survive these things at all cost. The remainder we already know. Yet these things leave their effect on other levels too. Trial makes man tough. It brings him a strength that otherwise he would not find. It highlights the better times and leads man to hope; to the hope of a better future and better times to come.

The other side of man is his spiritual self. Not the 'Hallelujah, praise the Lord' self, but the true essence of his own identity; his blueprint of himself.

Man is first and foremost an intelligent being of energy. Without this aspect he could not be alive. He could not manipulate the body that is his vehicle.

Man is part of a long chain of beings that are linked with him through his birth. This is his time to live, his window of opportunity to unleash the creative force that is present in him. This is his life.

Just for today, recognize the truth of yourself. Find the real you that exists within the automatic one. Send your thoughts up that you find the keys to unlock and unravel your full potential. Find the heritage that is only awaiting your recognition.

183
❖❖❖

I must learn to be firm when necessary.

Man thinks that to be good and kind means never to raise your voice and always say nice things, but that is wrong. All sides of life are equal. Positive and negative are equal. Light and dark, hot and cold, are all equal.

To take anger to one extreme is an imbalance, but to take niceness to the other is an equal imbalance. To look for the good is not an imbalance, but to see what is not really there, is.

The truth is always the bottom line. It can see what exists without colouration or extreme. The truth is neither nice nor unkind, it is not to be picky or a judge. The truth will be the guide to the reality of that which exists.

Just for today, keep life real. Be honest with yourself and open with those around you. Learn that you do have the right to speak your mind when necessary, appropriately. Learn to be firm, but kind, when the situation dictates. Ask always in thought for the words that are needed and that once given they may be understood.

184

◆◆◆

I must let others know how I think.

Every person has his own view of life. He has the truth as he knows it to be. Every truth is a record of life. It is a living record of a growing, living world.

Man walks this planet as its keeper, but also as its explorer and progressor. He touches his reality through creative expression and this he must pass onto others.

(I am I) The thoughts that you generate are the signals that are sent out to spirit. They dictate the things you next need, what you expect and your anticipated outcome. They tell us where you are in your understanding and progression and also connect you to the universal mind – to the God mind. Thoughts write the program of the life that you invent. (I am I)

Just for today, be aware of the thoughts that you generate. Share your mind with others who need the things you know. Allow them to share theirs with you and in return you may gain a truth that you need to grow forward.

185

◆◆◆

I must be able to act on the spur of a moment.

True expression is spontaneous. It is an instant response to the moment at hand.

For the majority of time, man operates on a slight delay system that allows him to plan his next move, his next words and his next days. This also gives him the ability to look forward and back through time, for its lessons and possible opportunities.

The whole of life would be void of challenge if the spur of the moment did not occur. Many can say that some best decisions were taken on a spur of the moment. The true light of creation is always accessible at these times.

Man must plan his life. To drift aimlessly day by day is to have no direction and to have no goal. But to stick too rigidly to plans is to suffocate in regime and regimentation. The light of life cannot shine through.

Just for today, allow yourself to make a snap decision. Allow the unwritten to come into play and take hold. You might be glad that you did.

186
❖❖❖

I must be mind-free of fear.

(I am I) The mind operates through a link system. This is built up through the whole of your life. The creative mind operates as a channel, a vessel for creative inspiration to flow through and express itself. (I am I)

Life cannot be creative for every individual, every moment of every day. Its basic necessities dictate repetitive patterns and acts of survival, but the life of a man means much more than this. Once his base requirements have been fulfilled, he is free to live and do as he pleases.

An open mind is able to operate without restriction and without set expectation. The closed mind exists only in its own parameter as it worries and frets about things that occur.

Just for today, understand that all your basic needs will be met. Yes, you must put things in order, but whatever you require will be available to you. Send your thoughts up to Source, and ask that your mind be bought back to peace. Ask that your life may unfold as it should, according to your needs and highest good.

187

❖❖❖

I must realize that my best effort is good enough.

The best effort of any man can only be according to his intelligence, ability and growth. He is limited only by his ability to achieve.

Man is full of intention and kindness of thought, but without the appropriate action, intention will count for nothing. Intention is a harvest of possibility that is waiting to be picked. It requires material action to manifest.

The manifestation of effort produces results, but again these can be hampered by a lack of confidence in the self. It is easy to believe you are not good enough, but the truth is that really you are.

Life is comprised of many levels, each with their own ceiling point of understanding. It takes many people to feel and update these levels. The efforts of none are ever a waste.

Just for today, as you look about, don't be pulled down by the achievements of others that seem to shade yours. It takes many people to effectively reach the corners and capabilities of life. You might help one or help thousands, but the point is that you help. Who can place a value on that?

188

❖❖❖

I must not let the anger of others get me down.

Your day is an open space. It is up to you how you fill it and what you choose to take on board.

The thoughts you have produce your mood of mind, but the moods of others can leave their effect also. The laughter of another will help lift you up, but their state of worry, stress and anger can bring you down and keep you there for a while.

Just for today, at the time that you must, place an imaginary cloak around yourself. Its colour must be green and it must reach the floor, to shield you. Ask quietly in thought that you be shielded from the negative vibrations of the mood swings of others. Ask that they also be brought back to peace and harmony, and that all they don't need be recycled.

189

❖ ❖ ❖

I must let the love of God help me – when I need to.

The love that God has for man requires no effort from him. It is natural.

(I am I) How could I not love that which belongs to me? Man is part of my body, of my own consciousness. How could I separate myself from myself? (I am I)

We all know our best side, but we know our downfalls even better. In fact, we know them so well that we keep them anchored to our backs as we drag them along. We know what we hide and we know we are unworthy – but wrong!

The things we did wrong we did in the past, at a time that we should have chosen better, but this is a new day, we keep on being told. It is a chance to step out of your shell. What you did wrong might still need to be put right, but sometimes it just isn't possible.

You are the product of all you have done, but you still have from now to go forward. You can be all that you wish, regardless of past. It is never too late to change tracks.

You are only held back by your opinion of self and are capable of being as good as you choose. You hold the key, but you must know that you are responsible for all that you become. You are as capable as the next man to live a good life and you are worthy, despite what you have done.

Just for today, recognize that you are always given two

chances at the very least. Allow the love of God, of Source, of the universal mind to guide you and point you in your best direction. Make each day a good day and soon your past will fall further and further away. You cannot always go back to the past to put it right, but you can choose to do better in the now.

190

❖❖❖

I will succeed.

No effort is ever a complete waste of time, and success is assured by greatness of the effort put in.

Your life, any life, is valuable. Every person is an equal part of the whole.

You are responsible for your life and so you must aim to succeed.

Just for today, recognize that this life is not a rehearsal. All that you do will take you to the next phase of your existence. You have your own mind and your own two hands and feet. Rely on no one but your own higher self and place order where chaos now reigns.

191

❖❖❖

I will be successful.

There is room for all in the world. The room and the right to shine is for everyone. Man needs recognition for his effort. He lives life to his highest ability and tries hard to achieve more than average. He is charitable and caring and he looks out for his neighbours and friends, but he can easily feel lost and abandoned.

Man has lost his faith in living and in life.

He imagines a heaven that is waiting. He would rather be there instead of here. The trust that he had once in life is now dwindling.

However, little does he know that he is already in heaven. He is the maker of his destiny – not God and not the people around about him. He must realize that he alone shapes his perception and world of matter, and what he contributes will help to form Earth planets future. He will leave behind his contribution as a legacy for generations still to come.

He cannot fail in this deed, because he forms part of the Earth. He will succeed in all that he chooses to do because that is his intention. Negativity, violence and fear will always attract and reproduce the same. Love and positive living will also.

Just for today, check the vibration you are living, choosing and sending out. There is nothing that can stop the law of cause and effect, except grace. You will succeed in the choices you make. Make sure that you will be proud of your outcome.

192

❖❖❖

I will help many people.

The nature of being human is to group. Even a loner will know other loners and that too will be much like a group.

The truth must always be exchanged, because only then can man be honest and open. When he lies or exaggerates with things that are not true, he is closed. The truth contains its own vital energy and this then reconnects back to life.

Man needs to be open to fulfil his purpose as a conductor and an energy channel. Whenever he communicates, energy will flow to him and from him with those he connects. This is his purpose in life. The input that we share is simply an energy transference. The energy we transfer is vital to the Earth and to life.

Man is the creator of now. Where his attention goes, energy flows. The point of energy transference is revitalization. Man replenishes resources when he pays attention to the subject in his now.

Just for today, recognize the higher purpose in your life. When you are open and true, there is nothing to worry about. The rest will happen naturally of its own accord, but when you are closed you become hard work. Others will find it draining to deal and integrate and spend company with you. Take the time to speak your truth and you will naturally help others in ways that you didn't even realize.

193

◆◆◆

I have God.

(I am I) The love that is, is God. The love that man feels is God. The feelings he feels as he looks out to sea, as he walks through the fields, or holds tight a loved one, are God. The love that flows through his being – all through his life – is God. God is the connection that gives life to life, and love to man. God is the beginning and God is the end. God is the energy that forms us and, combined, we are the energy that forms God. (I am I)

Man searches his whole life to find love, to receive love, to belong and to fit. He knows love as he lives out his choices; he knows love as he has a good day. He feels happy at the smallest of gestures and when other things work out as they should. When his life falls into place and everything flows, for a day, for a week or forever, it is because he has for that time at least, connected correctly to the life that is his and to the source of the love that is God.

God is not a person – that could not be. God is a name, the name of that which gives life. Some call it God, some Buddha, Allah, Krishna, Source or others still... There are as many different names and images as there are languages and countries on the planet. The name is unimportant, but the reality of God does exist.

Just for today, know that you are part of, and connected to God. Without that God link you could not be alive. God is the combined matter and consciousness of everything. God is a living, breathing reality, that is far greater than our human minds can yet perceive. You will never understand until suddenly you do, but never doubt that you are connected to God.

194

❖❖❖

I am not afraid to try something new.

Life is for living. The whole purpose of it is to experience, experiment, create and investigate.

The world existed before man. This planet was born and evolving long before man was even a part. Life will sustain itself, despite the things that man now thinks. This Earth is an intelligent, living organism in its own entirety.

(I am I) This Earth is my body, but man's own mind forms part of my consciousness. (I am I)

To live all through your life without growth or change is largely an impossibility. The very nature of life means change and growth.

Just for today, allow yourself to try something different, something new. Allow yourself to be as open and as willing to experiment as a child. This is your life, so enjoy the experience.

195

❖ ❖ ❖

I am happy.

Wanting to be happy and recognizing that you are, are two different things.

To be happy is to know happiness and the art of contentment in daily life. This sounds easy, but very few manage to achieve it at all. The art of being happy is to let life ebb and flow as it will. No one is immune from issues and circumstances, and once you know that these apply to all, you can be free to wade your way through them as they arise.

Happiness is the ability to clear your obstacles with the least amount of resistance.

(I am I. The only way to hold on to your happiness is to exist in a state of love, to keep an open, loving, easy frame of mind. This is the life you have chosen; not once, but with every decision, leading up to where you are now. You had the power to choose and you still do. You can choose and re-choose for the rest of your life. (I am I)

Just for today, recognize the power you have over yourself. You choose to be happy. You allow yourself to feel sad. Others can only upset you if you give them the power to do so.

196

❖ ❖ ❖

I must allow others to do as they would.

The choices you make in your own life are completely yours to be made, but so is it also with other people. They too are keepers of their own affairs.

To communicate and interact is the necessity of life. To live life for another is not.

The intelligence of man has many levels and thoughts, each with its floor and its ceiling. A child will begin at the base until it hits the ceiling of understanding for its age group or ability, then it will go up to a new level until it again hits the ceiling. This is normal growing practice for all.

Adults forget to grow. At some stage they merely survive. They become stuck in the mould they carve out for themselves and forget that more life exists.

Just for today, allow yourself to be yourself, and let others be all they want to be too. You can give them a nudge there and there, but ultimately this life is their own. The art of true friendship is helping and allowing each other the freedom to grow.

197

◆ ◆ ◆

I must be flexible.

The branch of the willow is supple, yet tough. It sways gently in the breeze, yet is very hard to break.

Life asks us to be as flexible as the willow, despite all the storms that rage along our path. When people remain stiff, they feel every bump and every pothole they encounter in their day. They are easily annoyed at distraction and when things interfere with their schedule. All issues seem high issues when they come into their path.

The other side of the coin is the ability to take life as it comes, in your stride. You know what needs doing, but if it happens out of sequence you don't mind. You remain unfazed. The ability to bend with life's current is yours.

Just for today, bend like the willow. Remain open and flexible. Keep your ears and eyes open and look out to help others who are not as accommodating as you. Help them with thought rather than deed. Send your thoughts out to the God mind that their needs may be met to bring them back to balance and to peace.

198

***

I must not be afraid to shout when necessary.

Man was given the gift of speech. How he then uses it will depend on his state of mood and mind.

To communicate is the most important thing, but to do it well is an art that needs to be worked at. Words mix up with feelings; emotion and intention also get in the way. The more we explain, it seems the less we are understood.

Understanding is a problem that words can find hard to address, as they are too limiting. Finding the correct ones to accurately portray the need can be difficult. Words are also easily forgotten; once spoken they disappear; they are history.

(I am I) Words alone have little meaning. It is the intention, action and clout behind them that carry them home. (I am I)

Just for today, remember that you don't always have to be quiet and meek. When something needs saying, say it - but with love. Love will always keep all things in check. When you need to shout, do it, but with no more than the situation itself dictates.

(I am I) The words spoken must be truth – without insult or colouration. (I am I)

199

◆◆◆

I must play my part, then leave others to play theirs as they should.

A computer works window by window. All options are always available, but the ones chosen depend on the project in hand and the individual knowledge of the operator.

Life is the same – without exception.

The very nature of life is to create, to grow and to change. This occurs daily with every passing moment. All over the world individuals are living and creating their reality, step by step. Things will run well when they occur as they should, but when a problem arises it is the same as a traffic jam. The life flow of the individual or individuals concerned will get bumpy – or grind to a stop.

(I am I). When a blockage occurs it is a way of saying that the issue or problem needs tuning. Problems get our attention. They help us clear space and grow forward. They keep things in good working order. (I am I)

Just for today, take care of your affairs. Take advice or give it when necessary, then move on. Take time to unblock or clear out and allow others to do so too. Send your thoughts to the God mind, to Source, and ask for the help that you need – for the highest good. Ask that peace and love be paramount.

200

❖ ❖ ❖

I must be better than others around me.

(I am I) I am the light. I am brighter than your eyes could look upon. You are part of me, so you also carry the light – my light. The brightness of your light is not as strong as it could be, because it is shrouded by your deeds of life. The light can never snuff out, but it can become brighter or dimmer, according to your adventure. You keep it dim or clear with your intentions and action. (I am I)

To be better than others around you is to go your own way in truth and love and sincerity. It is easy to follow a trend, even when you don't really agree.

Just for today, be a pioneer. The best in you is waiting to come forth, so allow it the space to do that. Send your thoughts out up high and ask to be helped in the necessary way to achieve your highest good. The intentions you carry will do the rest.

201

❖ ❖ ❖

I am happy to be alive.

When you understand the importance of being here, you will welcome your new days with joy. Not an uncontrolled euphoria, but the joy of what this day will bring.

The whole of a day will not be enough to experience and

achieve all you wish. Ask for your perception of time to slow down, that it be stretched as long as possible so you can use it at your leisure.

The day you are now experiencing is the start of the rest of your life. Tidy it up as much as you can and take care of the seeds that you set.

Just for today, recognize the unique opportunity you are in. You have the chance to straighten things out and move on.

202

❖❖❖

I must leave my past as it is. There is no room for regrets.

(I am I) The past is over. The future is just a dream. Today is the place that creates and causes matter. Today is your only reality. (I am I)

You are being asked not to spoil the day you are now experiencing. All your yesterdays were once a day such as this. The things you did, whether by choice or necessity, whether under your own direction or the force of another, were the outcome of the place in life you were at then.

Hindsight offers many opinions. It is easy to look back with joy or regret, but if you knew the definite outcome of everything, you would not be free to create, to choose, to live. All that you are now, is because of and despite of your past. All that you have been through has brought you to this point. You are a work in progress – not yet the finished article itself.

Just for today, let your past rest as it will. Send your thoughts to the God mind, to Source, and ask that old pain, regret and guilt be recycled. Ask that you be free to move on. This day is a gift. Don't pull the past forward to relive it and give it new life; instead enjoy the time you are in. Live it for all you are worth.

203

❖❖❖

I must learn to look at today without the pull of the past or the future.

The power of thought is the creative intelligence at work.

Where thought flows, energy goes. We bring life to the images in our head.

To think constantly about past events is to live them over and over again. You feed them and keep them alive. While this is fine for good times and events of our choice, it is not fine for painful experiences. Let the pain be gone. You cannot alter what has already occurred, but you can re-choose your attachment to it. Let the negativity be recycled until you can access those memories without attachment. You are the one who lived them, but you don't have to drag them with you forever.

To be too obsessed with the future is to live in constant illusion. The future is a dream until you get there, until it becomes the now. When you are frightened or nervous, you place negative energy at that point ahead in real time. When you finally get there, you will feel all the doubt that you sent. When you are overexcited, you wish your life away. You place too much hype at the time of the event, so how could it live up to the hype of expectations? You will have built it up too high, and by wishing it to come sooner the experience will fly by too fast. You will have robbed yourself of its pleasure.

Just for today, keep your mind clear and focused on today. Enjoy every moment without anticipation and expectation. Have the time at hand as it occurs.

204

❖ ❖ ❖

I must live each day as it comes.

(I am I) Today is a new day. It will need its own care and attention to detail. Many influences will alter and priorities will fluctuate. You must pay attention to all that crosses your path or your field of focus. This is my request to you. (I am I)

Your field of vision and attention is unique to you. You have been trained by your lifetime experiences to behave and act how you do. You know what is acceptable behaviour and what is not. You play your part in the corner of the world you interact with. You talk with your mouth and you see with your eyes. You are a receiver for the world to mediate through.

The role you play is important. When care and attention to detail is perfected within your own life you are also able to highlight when others need help in the now they effect.

Just for today, keep your own life on track. Be focused and vigilant in the roles that are yours. When you sense the alarm bells of others, send out your thoughts. Ask that all unnecessary negativity be removed and recycled. Ask that the help they need in their now time be given – for the highest good of the situation and individuals concerned. You must ask for help on their behalf and then you must opt to let go.

205

❖ ❖ ❖

I take with me the promise of my future.

The mindset you have will dictate the future you attract.

(I am I) Man has the gift of free will, and with that come personal choice and direction. The mind is not your master. Instead it waits for direction and guidance from you. Like a small child that is incapable of fending for itself, the mind will wander aimlessly wherever it can until you take it firmly by the reins. (I am I)

Life is hard, but it is equally happy. When you are happy inside yourself, trouble is more easily overcome.

The future of man is waiting to be written. All that he wants is within his grasp, but to access it he needs an open and uncluttered state of mind.

Just for today, know that your luck is as good as you make it. Take this day and use it for all of its worth. The future will be fine just as long as you take care of now.

206

❖ ❖ ❖

I must live life to the full.

The fullness of life has a different meaning to everyone.

There are people who plod consistently and slowly through their day. These are the backbone of society. They can be relied upon to always do the things that they do. They need repetition and little change, because then they feel most secure. The whole of their life may be lived the same way. They are happy as long as they are left alone.

There are people who just cannot settle down, whether in house or in job or in partner. They lack security and roots. They try many things, but cannot feel connected and at one.

There are people who invite change and experience into their life. They will try all that they come across, just because they can, they live for each moment without undue thought of past or future, enjoying now.

The world will make provision for all. Wherever you fit, whatever you like and think; it will open up the avenues you ask of it.

Just for today, live your time to its fullest. If opportunity presents something that you might like to try – then do it now. This is your life, your time and your journey – so enjoy it.

207

❖❖❖

I must let life unfold as lovingly as it can.

Life is a positive experience. It is as loving and accommodating as you allow it to be.

The most important thought to remember is that like attracts like. Negative thought and action will only produce more of the same. Positive intention will punch through negativity as though it was not really there. Positive thought will produce matter that works in its favour. It will open the avenues that will take you safely towards your next set of possibilities and options.

Just for today, remain in the energy of love. Let life unfold without force or undue manipulation. All that is yours and all that you need, will come into your court as it should. Stay open and allow it to be.

208

❖❖❖

I will survive all that I have to endure.

All stress and trauma are symptomatic of a phase that will pass. Each moment or event must continue until it is through.

Life is a natural state of constant flux. It must be, or it could not be alive. Without the good we could not know bad, and without them there would not be any growth.

The whole of nature must endure its cycles of birth, of growth and of decay, and once they are past it must begin all over again.

There can be no beginning without first the end – the end of what was is now over.

Just for today, recognize that nothing and nobody can harm you. They might cause you to hurt, in more ways than one, but you will always survive the experience. You will gain strength of character despite their efforts. You will grow as otherwise you could not have done. When all is over, thank them. Send your thoughts out to God, and thank them for the lessons that now are behind you.

209
❖ ❖ ❖

I am living my truth.

(I am I) The truth is the whole version of yourself, without discrimination. (I am I)

The truth is the version of yourself that you alone know you are. It is the face that is you without need for edit. It's the thoughts that you carry, that reflect on the face that you show. There is nothing hidden and nothing to be taken away.

Very few individuals can travel through life without collecting garbage. They make mistakes, often whoppers, that in hindsight they wish they had not. In the true light of who you are, nothing can be hidden. There is nowhere to hide our soul's blueprint.

Man's biggest fear is that someone, at some time, either in this life or in the next, will judge him. He fears that he will be recognized for all the wrongs he has done. Because of this he digs himself in even deeper. He adds wrong to wrongs, because he fears being caught if he breaks up the cycle. He is not really happy in the place that is his, but he fears moving forward even more.

Just for today, recognize the true value of yourself. This is a new day so let go of fear, of outdated beliefs and of ropes that keep you pinned down. You are the only one that can stop these old patterns.

210
❖❖❖

I am living in the light of eternal love.

The light of the creator exists in all matter. The Earth is matter, the natural world is matter, and man is part of that matter.

The light of the world plays a part through man. Light is energy and energy is light. Man is a mixture of matter, energy and light.

Light that is energy cannot snuff itself out. It can be blocked, diverted or spent, but it cannot put itself out.

The deeds of man can darken his light. He can shield it with armour strengthened through wrong, but he can never, ever, extinguish it completely. It is not his to put out. He is part of the body of God, and his light is his connection to the energy and love of his source.

The body of man is grown by man. It is formed to live his physical experience. The soul of a man is connected to God and God is the combination of all.

Just for today, understand that you are forever connected to the love that is God. Nothing can alter it. Know that you are the light, you carry that light, so live in the light that is you.

211

❖❖❖

I am steadily moving closer to God.

Every soul is a work in progress: Each is on a journey to perfection.

No soul can regress. The life that you live will endow you with learning. Like a child, it will grow from experience.

The hope is that somewhere along the way each individual will wake up to the reality of the life that is his.

(I am I) The reality is his connection to the planet itself. To the contribution he was destined to make. (I am I)

When man does not wake up he will live through his life and think himself alone. He will struggle and fret and try his best, but he will not connect with the help at his hand. At the end of his days he will finally go home, richer for his experience, but not as full and as happy as he could have been. He will have neither regressed nor progressed. He will have stayed practically the same.

Just for today, recognize the value of growth in your own life. Ask that you be given the help to move up and on with your learning. Look for the light that lies hidden from view and work slowly and steadily towards it.

212

❖❖❖

I will be all that I am supposed to be.

(I am I) The purpose of man is to live and experience life to the full. Each will be given the necessary tools to do so. (I am I)

The building blocks of a life must be laid firm, solid and straight. This will determine mans basic posture and identity in life. He then adds to these blocks everyday that he lives through experience and communication and learning. All that is his will always be forthcoming. He need neither fight nor manipulate to gain it.

Many life cycles are born and ended during the course of an Earthly existence. Man will choose and re-choose, swap and change many times. This is the way of growth of evolution. This is his purpose on Earth.

Just for today, remember that you cannot be all you are supposed to be, until you know clearly what you are not. All that is yours will always be with you until you need it no longer. You have all the help of the universe at your disposal, so be open enough to receive it now.

213

◆◆◆

I must take turmoil as easily as I am able to.

No one enjoys trouble or, even less, pain. Turmoil and change can inflict pain on a deep emotional level.

Worry and problems are things that nudge life back on course. They highlight issues that need addressing and changing, because something was missed or overlooked along the way. They help us to grow, take stock and clear out our rubbish, as we are forced to stop and pay greater attention.

To always follow the trend of the many is easy, but offers little growth or excitement. Then because it is monotonous, you don't pay full attention and can miss your own signposts that alert that a problem is brewing.

(I am I) The turmoil that you feel is just a passing phase. It simply needs realignment with the world at large. Hand your problems up to me and I will help you find the solution that is best at this time. You must do the groundwork, but I will help things slot into place where I can. The picture that you see is not always the completed version. I will help you find the answers. (I am I)

Just for today, embrace your problems and solve them easily and efficiently. The new direction is waiting for you to find it.

214

❖❖❖

I must help others over and beyond their milestones as I, too, was once helped by Source.

(I am I) All of humanity is linked by the fact that together they formulate their part of my body, of my consciousness and my existence. They join with me to formulate one. (I am I)

Throughout life, when help is needed, the universe will find a way to get it to you: It will use whatever means becomes available at the time.

The evolution of man is on an even course. Many people will experience the same things simultaneously. Many will face similar problems and cross similar bridges. Each person will either consciously or subconsciously gather the necessary information from another. Many will help each other without request or prompt – the way it should be.

When a blockage arises many will experience the problem, but no one can as yet find the solution. This is the time that God, that Source, will step in. The universe will always come to our rescue, provided we remain still enough with our mind to receive it.

Just for today, recognize the times you have been invisibly helped. Recognize that once you have found a solution, others will be placed in your path to share the same thing. You are now in a position to help, through the experience and knowledge that was given to you. Link your thoughts to the God mind, to Source, that all may be as it should.

215

❖❖❖

I must not be too rigid in my daily plans, so that life can flow freely, just as it should.

Life needs time to breathe, to set seed and to grow.

The people of the 21st century have forgotten how to wait and be patient. Because all things are available at the push of a button or the flick of a switch, when the response is not instantaneous they think that something is wrong. To wait is no longer a part of their natural behaviour.

Life must take its own time. It will not be hurried; it cannot be rushed. Nothing can be born before the time it is ready.

The time of man is precious. Once it is spent it is gone forever. Days are planned in advance in detail, just to make them more productive. Just to make life fit.

Just for today, do all that you must, but leave the room for your life to manoeuvre. Allow little things to come into play before you rush to the next phase. Take the time to grasp and feel this day that is yours.

216

❖❖❖

I must let life order me around once in a while.

Life cannot be hurried and each thing has its place, but once in a while it is necessary to quicken its pace.

Man is most comfortable working at his own pace. He knows his priorities and the time he has available, but sometimes his pace can be misjudged. Sometimes he must quicken to meet the next stage that is waiting for him to connect.

The life that you see is only one part of the picture. Just like a movie, there is a lot of planning, work and movement behind the scene. Man is the vehicle that pulls everything together in the now – at the time that is correct and is needed.

Just for today, allow life to dictate the pace. Go with the flow, whether it is fast or slow. You control the time of your physical now, but life must connect with you too.

217
❖❖❖

I will do all that I can to help others.

To help means to give of yourself without giving too much away of yourself, or to give without cost to yourself other than that which you are prepared to give.

To give is to make yourself available at any time that is necessary, but also to remain in your truth. If something does not fit, then it was not meant to be. Let go and allow the seeker to turn to their next option. By remaining honest you have allowed the correct help to filter through in its rightful place.

To be open and honest with yourself as well as others gives

life a chance to kick in when it needs to.

Man learns from an early age how good it feels to help another, always, yet often his input is inappropriate or unnecessary.

Always be available when your help is requested, and when you can assist, that is good, but we can often go too far out of our own way, in a direction that did not fit the bill in the first place. In an effort to be nice, we can create more confusion, so the trick is to be honest from the start.

No two people are ever alike and neither are the roots of their problems. Their solutions may vary considerably too.

The universe will take care of us all, if only we could let go a bit and let it. Sometimes it is ok to say no.

Just for today, if you have the solution, then use it, if you have time then fine, but if not, then be open and honest. Your truth is worth more than you know. Instead send your thoughts up to God mind, to Source, as your friend walks away, that they may quickly find the connection they need. In letting go, you allow life to step in.

218
❖❖❖

I will not question too deeply what I am being asked to do by God, by Source.

(I am I) The word of God is always loving. Never will it provoke negative action, fear, fighting or pain. The word of God will

stand up to scrutiny. It stands for all that is truth. (I am I)

God is the combination of all that exists on this planet. The Earth is its physical body. The consciousness of all combines in Heaven and Earth, to form the consciousness that is God.

God has no arms and legs of his own – he has many. He has not two ears or one mouth – he has many. God has the use of every human being, every animal and every object on the planet. He has the use of the elements. He has the span of time. All that God is, and even more, he can use through the channels that are available – especially through the channels that are us.

When a signal for help goes out, God must use any means in 'our' power and intelligence to deliver the help that is necessary.

Just for today, remain open but focused on your task at hand. Only when you are relaxed can you listen to the thoughts that may be placed in your mind. Once you are in tune with life you allow yourself to be a vessel, a channel for the universe to make the connections it must. You are the hands and the eyes and the ears that may be used when the opportunity arises. You are a tool for God when he needs you. You trust God and God trusts you. You are one with the world that exists.

219

❖ ❖ ❖

I will be.

How many different hats do you wear in a day?

(I am I) I must wear the greatest number of all, as I am all things to all people. (I am I)

How many heads must you wear on your shoulders?

(I am I) I must wear the greatest number of them all. (I am I)

How many times do you take them all off?

(I am I) I never can! (I am I)

Just for today, relish the times that you can just be yourself; the times that you simply can 'be'. Realize how lucky you are! Be thankful that you can and be proud of the self that you own.

220

❖ ❖ ❖

I am the Son of God.

Man need be neither martyr nor saint. He is loved for the person he is.

(I am I) The whole of your world is an invention. It was made because of somebody's dream. (I am I)

Think about your own life – the one you have known since your childhood. Every step that you took was because either you or someone else thought that you should, that it would be best, that it would make you happy, somehow in some way.

But what if there was more to life than meets the eye? What if there really was a God that loved you and cared for your well being?

You really are the Son of God. You are the creator of the life you display.

Just for today, think about the implications of being man. Think about how you have lived until now and then think of the time yet to come.

221

❖❖❖

I am the light of the world.

(I am I) There are two trains of thought – light and dark. I am the light – the truth and the love. All other thoughts reflect shades of dark. This is all that there is. (I am I)

All that man is and all that he does must fit into one category or the other. If like attracts like, he is either positive or negative in nature. Every act undertaken combines matter with energy to make form. Man creates his own reality from the light and dark waves that he makes.

(I am I) Man must be more aware of the thoughts and patterns

he generates. With every second that passes he is creating the world he perceives and surveys. All that he does in his own life he will add to the world as a whole. He adds negativity with thoughts of anger and condemnation, and this adds even more to the unrest of the world, to the unrest he feels inside of himself. (I am I)

Just for today, send out nothing but love. When someone angers you, recycle it and ask that they feel love, light and balance instead. When the news headlines are frightening, ask for the whole thing to be recycled, ask that love reach the situation instead. When you would normally stress or worry, ask that you remain calm and at peace. Add nothing but love to diffuse the situations you witness.

To be in the love means you operate from within the light. By remaining there consciously you send light to the troubles of the world as they happen. You are helping to disperse the darkness. Ask with your thoughts for whatever is needed. Only you have control of the now.

222

❖❖❖

I must have patience with life.

To be patient means to be able to wait.

The people of the world vary greatly in character, speed and intelligence. This is necessary to cover the many levels of energy transference needed to maintain life on this Earth.

Man performs a much wider role with his actions than is often immediately apparent. By his interaction he sustains this world on many levels.

It is usual to speed through many things, but we must also allow for the differences of others. When man pushes forward too fast, he can miss the connections required.

Just for today, recognize that the many levels of speed in the world are necessary. Allow others the time for their interaction, and allow yourself to slow down a bit too. Give life its chance to keep up.

223

❖❖❖

I must have patience with myself.

(I am I) Life was created in days, but those days took millions of years in your time. I had to wait for each stage to complete before I could work on the next. (I am I)

No man can beat time, but his perception of time can alter greatly – depending on the state of his mind.

Man is energy and matter. Matter vibrates at a much slower pace than its original energy form. When man is happy his vibration level quickens. He can whiz through a day and wonder where time has gone. When he is down his vibration slows. An hour can seem like three as it looms ahead in front of him.

Man is just waking up to the reality of his interaction with life. He is learning to manage his mind and his thoughts at a more conscious level of understanding. He is learning the different ways that he connects to the world that integrates and operates around him.

Just for today, be patient with yourself. It is not easy to unlearn what was always automatic. Each time you slip, allow yourself to return to the moment at hand. Remain focused and balanced on your now and all other things will come back into place.

224
❖❖❖

I am living my life to the full, at every opportunity that I am presented with.

The pleasure of life is to be free to live it at any opportunity given.

When you take up a chance, then go with the flow, let things unfold as they will.

Just for today, be spontaneous. Let your hair down and enjoy your day. You might even make a memory or two.

225

❖❖❖

I am an instrument of God, of Source; a bringer of light, of laughter and of peace.

(I am I) You are unique. You have been perfectly crafted to fit the mould of your life. You are living the now of creation. You have my body – your world – at your feet. (I am I)

You spread energy wherever you go. You carry life to the rest of the world. You are making connections that life deems you should – very well.

Just for today, allow the magnificence of life to create through you. You need be nothing more than your natural self. Stay in the truth and out of illusion - and let laughter and upliftment flow.

226

❖❖❖

I am happy in the life I am in.

(I am I. When you can sit down and smile, life is good. When you can be open and honest, life is good. When you have nothing to hide and nothing to fear, you are living life as you should. (I am I)

The life you live must be your most prized possession. You have all that you need at your feet.

If you are not happy, then find out why. Look to see where changes are to be made, but in love, without anger or force. Look to see what is hurting and send your thoughts out to God mind, to Source. Ask for some help to pinpoint the problem, and ask for the solution to come easily too.

Just for today, realize the importance of being happy and at one with your surroundings. Take care of your commitments and do what you must, but be happy in the life that is you.

227

❖❖❖

I must be able to look at my past without wishing I was still in it.

Life ticks past in stages. There are definite chapters, highs and lows, to be seen.

Each chapter of life contains what you need and attract at the time you are in it, each one is important, to take your soul forward in experience, expression, learning and progression. You helped create it, through needs, wants, agendas, desires, thoughts and intentions you carried.

Outside influences will come and go; they may leave their mark, they may not. Again, how much you feel it will depend on you too. You can only be hurt when you allow pain on board. You can protect yourself more than you know. You have control of your thoughts and your actions, but you cannot control the behaviour or intent of other people. They just do as they do. You can control, however, the way you choose to take things on board in your own mind.

The rest of your life is trying to unfold – let it.

The past is the vehicle that has brought you to now. You are all that you are, despite it; because of it. The good and the bad have been and gone. Don't give it new life with your live energy of the now. Let it fall away as it must, and if this is hard – don't forget to ask for help. Send your thoughts out to the God mind, to the Source you're part of, and ask for it all to be lifted. It will be recycled for your own highest good. Ask as often as you need to until you can look back without feeling pain – or wishing that you were still there.

Just for today, recognize the power of your own mind and its thoughts. Remain in your now and allow creation to take you forward to the place that was yours all along.

228

❖❖❖

I will not try to pre-empt information that is not quite mine to know yet.

We all do it! We just find it so hard to wait!

Energy flows where thought and information go; nothing can be born before its time. By needing to know
everything in advance, we rob ourselves of its unfolding experience. We rob energy from the surprise, from the actual birth of the event itself.

Just for today, wait. Wait for what you can hardly wait for. Let it come in the time that it will.

229
❖❖❖

I will busy myself with today's tasks that I have set.

You have a plan in your head of things that you must do or want to achieve. You must stick to it, in order to complete it.

All you can place behind you will clear your path for the future. You will feel freer and lighter than you have done for ages, just because you have unblocked your souls path way – to allow some new energy in.

Just for today, get going. Finish some things on your list.

230
❖❖❖

I must keep both the physical and the spiritual in perfect balance within myself.

The body of man is composed of matter – to form the vehicle that moves the soul, the spirit, the eternal part of himself. The spiritual self is energy. It is a perfect copy of your life and your physical self. It is also the blueprint of the whole of your individual existence and journey through time.

The spiritual needs the physical to operate and experience a life of matter on the planet that we live upon. Without the physical body we could not interact the in way that we want to with life. We could not have the experience of life that we do now on planet Earth.

Both the physical body and the spiritual one hold equal importance to man. Both must co-exist in perfect balance to enjoy good health, harmony and wellbeing. When one part goes out of sync, man experiences discomfort, energy drain, lethargy or illness. He must take some time out to nurture himself back to wholeness, to rebalance the two parts that are him.

Just for today, take notice of how you feel. If you are unwell, then correct it. If you are happily balanced and content, then recognize that you are and be thankful. Either way, send your thoughts upstairs back to Source, and talk to the ones who are helping, assisting, unseen. Have trust in the help that is with you.

231
❖❖❖

I must keep myself physically balanced at all times.

The physical is your mode of existence at this time.

The balance of the physical needs more than just balance of diet and body; more important than all is a balance of mind. To remain in the now instead of past and future is balance. To be receptive to the moment is balance. To be open and honest to the point of transparency is balance. To remain in the love without suspicion or fear is balance. To accept all that life deals without undue stress or resistance is balance.

Just for today, take note of your physical balance. Think about how many times you allow your balance to tip. Life will take you in many directions, but the more you can bring yourself back to peace, the quicker, easier and more natural a state of balance will become. Gradually you will retain it – even when you might be cross. You will respond to every moment with truth and love and openness. You will be at one with yourself, with Earth and life.

232
❖❖❖

I must let others tell me their problems so that I have a better understanding of how best to help them.

It is easy to talk to others, but how many of us actually listen and correctly hear the words being said?

People pass on information, that's what they do.

(I am I) It is how the world operates and interconnects. It is one way of energy transference. (I am I)

The problem is that too many of us are locked into the self. We are wrapped up and caught up in our own little worlds. We live in the pain of our thoughts. We hear what we think is being said, instead of the words being used. We fill in the blanks and take things to mean what we want them to mean. We are lead by emotion and illusion rather more than reality itself

Just for today, allow yourself to listen. Take a back seat and hear the world about you. You may be surprised at how refreshing this can be. You may be surprised at what you will learn.

233

❖ ❖ ❖

I must learn that to grieve is a natural part of the healing of pain.

We think of grief as a natural part of the loss of a loved one, but life has many endings that must be experienced and expressed.

Whenever a door opens it must eventually close to allow for growth and for change. Problems arise when we get caught in the comfort zone, when we prefer to stay where we are, because it feels familiar and sure. Change can feel uncertain and that will lead to insecurity and fear. We often stay far too long at an outgrown stage, because we fear to step away from its security.

Life, however, needs the opposite. To truly experience it head-on, man needs to be open and not fearful. He can only create when he allows himself the space to create with. Living a life of security may feel better, but where is the option to grow? How can you fulfil your dreams, when you are too frightened to step away from the usual things that you do?

Just for today, when the end of a cycle approaches, allow yourself to let it come. Know it is natural to grieve the loss of the familiar and that it helps in the process of clearing out and letting go. Know that whenever the sun sets it must also rise again, because this is the nature of life. Remember also to send your thoughts out to God mind, to Source. Ask that you be given the help you need to allow this phase to pass, and to grow. You are a work in progress that must allow the next phase to come in.

234
❖❖❖

I must always hand my pain up to God, to Source, to take away and recycle.

The day is fresh and unwritten. Any fear or pain, stress or anxiety left over from yesterday must not gain fresh hold in the now. This day is to live – not to fear.

The gift of life is precious, but it also comes with a price. To experience it properly you must be free of unnecessary clutter. You must relinquish what you no longer need.

Yesterday is spent. It was once a page just like this, but it is now written up, used and sealed. All that occurred must remain there, because there is where it belongs. It forms the window of what has now passed.

Do you want to remould this day in the same way? Do you want its copy?

Just for today, let the pain of the past go. It has performed its function. All that was done cannot be undone, but you need not give it yet more precious fresh life. You need not bring it forward into this day – into your now.

Life is full of mistakes, but to add to them is a senseless act and a waste. Send your thoughts out to God and ask for it all to be recycled. Ask that yesterday's residue be rendered null and void in the present. Only you can decide to let the rubbish go, or you will simply carry it on – to mar the future.

235

❖ ❖ ❖

I will address each issue at the time that it arrives in my day.

The moment you are in has never been experienced before. It is new and open to all possibilities of life. It is only here that every option is available and at your disposal. It is only here that you can access the full force of creation itself.

Think of the years you have now been alive. Then think of the days and the hours. Now calculate further and think of the minutes and moments those represent. Each one was unique and precious; you chose each one either directly or indirectly. Yet how often did you feel you were free to create? How often did others lead you, by the past, or by what you thought the outcome 'should' have been? How often did you really explore the other options available at the time?

Just for today, be open. Be like a blank canvas, waiting to be turned into its picture. How can you know the outcome of what has never before been experienced? This day is not the same as the past; so don't paint it as though it were. Send your thoughts out and ask that this day be lived for its own worth, and for its highest good.

236

❖❖❖

I must be open to the suggestion of the moment I am dealing with.

The nature of creation is without limitation. It is to be without expectation of outcome through the manipulation of force. To be creative is to go with the flow of the moment at hand.

Just for today, be simply in the moment. Allow life to take you forward instead of rushing there yourself. Follow the leads that manifest.

237

❖❖❖

I must be lively when the situation requires it.

Energy travels in bursts and waves. The energy of life flows much the same way. Distinct patterns will lift us high and pull us down. The trick is to recognize which wave you are on.

Man is an energy conductor. He can add to a situation, balance it, disrupt it or finalize it. He does much that he does not even know.

Just for today, try to remain open and neutral. Approach all you come across from a different point of view. What are you adding or removing by your attention? Is your presence really required, or do you simply feel the need to be involved? If you are unsure send your thoughts out and ask for any assistance required.

238

❖❖❖

I must be able to enforce the boundaries that I put into place.

Life is full of rules and regulations. Some are helpful while others are not. For convenience it can be simple to place boundaries where there really should be none. It is also evident that we let things slip here and there, because we cannot be bothered to enforce the more bothersome regulations that are necessary to keep things in order.

Just for today, be aware of the boundaries you place upon others and equally those that are expected of you. Look behind what is taken for granted and see if there is room for improvement, growth or change. Ask silently for advice or any help and understanding that is needed.

239

❖ ❖ ❖

I am only one small voice, one small energy, within one small person, but these in themselves represent the light of the world.

The truth behind the words you have just read cannot be visible from the position of your vision. To see the truth you must know the outcome — and this you will not until the end of your life span.

Individually, man is small. He is fairly insignificant in the scale of the world, yet also he is not. Each man lies at the centre of his own universe. The ripples he sends out will be felt by many and in turn he will affect the lives of everyone he touches, whether he knows it or not.

(I am I) All life is part of the one life that is God. When man lives according to the law of the universe, I will magnify all that he does, from one to then 500 times. When he works with truth and light he works in my name; in my image. When he works to better the life of his fellow man, with all his heart and love, I will better his best effort, because he then does it in my name. (I am I)

Just for today, realize the power of the actions you take, the words you speak and the thoughts you generate.

(I am I) You become the creator in place of me. You have all the power of the world at your disposal, so learn to wield it well. (I am I)

240

❖❖❖

I must not stumble under the weight that I feel I must carry. I must instead hand these things up and back to Source.

The weight that you carry is not the weight of matter, but of mind.

The mind when it is troubled is the heaviest burden of all. It can kill a man dead when he cannot bring it to peace. It can cause more illness and heartache, war and destruction than many can imagine today.

The burden of the mind must be handed over to God. Ask with your thoughts that all you need not carry be lifted. Ask that your mind can be brought back to peace.

Just for today, recognize that your thoughts are signals, and your link with creation and energy keeps them alive. Thoughts create your reality. Be careful of where you allow them to wander. Be careful to keep them clear and focused in the moment you are experiencing.

241

❖ ❖ ❖

I am in complete balance.

Balance is the point of the truth of creation.

(I am I) It is where you will always find the help that is waiting to manifest in your life. (I am I)

The point of balance is that you will live neither in one direction or another too heavily. It is the place of life where all things are equal and all things are possible. The right balance must be kept in all walks of life to retain order properly.

Man is able to do all that he wants. He can dream, he can choose and he can activate. He has complete power over all he surveys, but he must think about the cause and then its effect. The right choices made at the right time will keep his life in well-balanced order. All things will run smoothly and correct connections will be met. But if he leans too heavily in any one direction he will offset the balance of another. Then he must play the catch-up game to get back on track once more.

Just for today, check your own state of balance. Are all your life sections up to date? Do others chase you for things left undone, or do you find the need to chase them? The balance of home, of work, of recreation and of sleep is as important as the balance of nature. When you are out of sync at all, you take order twice away from your life, once to catch up and once to get back to where you should be. Find the balance to restore what you must and ask for the help that you need.

242

◆◆◆

I have achieved all that I set out to do.

The truth of life is to live and experience and enjoy.

When you can stand tall with your hand on your heart and know you have done your best, then you are living your life in the truth. When you know you could or should have done better, then there is room for improvement.

The secret to a good life is not material and social wealth, but wealth of the heart and peace of mind. The things that you set out to do might not be the most important for humanity, but simply the best in your own world. When you can make people happy; when you can right a wrong; when you live fully in the role of your connection to others, you are living your purpose. When you can look back at the end of a day and be pleased with its outcome, you are living your life, as you should.

Just for today, realize that little things hold most importance in the day-to-day running of the world. Try to achieve at least one thing in everyday and soon you will no longer have to try. All you set out to do you will finish.

243

❖❖❖

I am at my best when I am helping others.

The truth is that very few people are immune to the feelings of dislike felt by others.

(I am I) Man was conceived in love. He was born into a loving environment and has known love at most stages of his growing life. He is love. He feels comfortable and at one with love. When he finds himself in a situation of no love – or, even worse, alienation - it feels uncomfortable and unnatural to his being. He tries to find out why and put it right. At his most basic level he needs acceptance for his own internal well-being. (I am I)

When man is well and whole he is happy. When all his needs are met, he looks outward to share the good fortune that he feels. He wants others to feel as he does. He has a need to help his fellow man in the best way that he knows how.

Until we learn otherwise, we can only help with the tools that we have at hand – our friendship, our time-sharing, our possessions and advice. The majority would give the shirt off their back to help another who is failing. That is the nature of unconditional love. That is the essence of sharing and community. That is the brotherhood of man.

Just for today, recognize that there is nothing you can do that will take the place of love and true kindness. The true light of the force that lives through fellow man will always outshine the onset of turmoil. Ask with your thoughts for all that is needed and know that you are best when you feel useful.

244

❖ ❖ ❖

I will not doubt what has proven to be true.

The experiences of your life are perfectly true to you because you have lived them, experienced them and know them without shadow of doubt.

All people have their own truths. Some will be as yours and others will vary greatly. No one is less or more important than another. All truths will reflect a section or part of the whole, but all that is known is not all that there is to be known, it is just what is known right now.

The knowledge of man is growing to greater heights than he could have previously imagined, but again it can only gain the height of information available to him. Man tries too hard to learn secrets that matter, when they were part of his mind all along.

Just for today, keep your mind open and clutter free. All that you need will be placed in your path. Your questions and desires are known. Your purpose is already waiting for your own recognition. You know the truth that you have lived and the way that you are heading. Believe in your potential that is unfolding.

245

❖ ❖ ❖

I will believe the best that I am.

(I am I) You are a being of energy and light. You are a human being. You are a being that is individual. You are important just because you are you.

All that you have been before does not matter. The mistakes you have made do not matter. There is nothing that could make me disconnect from you. You simply thought that I had.

Take this day and the rest of your life to be the version of the being that is your true likeness. Be the highest vibration and version of the self you are able to be.

This is my pledge to you: I will never let you down; I will never let you go; I will always know your smallest thought, and I will never hold your past against you.

Just for today, know that I am not a fairy tale. You are as real as me. If I were not real, then you could not be – for you are a part of my body, of my mind, of my love and creative potential. You are a part of a living breathing entity that is life. (I am I)

246

◆◆◆

I will achieve the best that I aim to believe in.

Your mind is yours to conduct. Only you can choose what it will feast on. Only you can allow it to roam. You control its hold over you and also what it creates.

Two and two make four. Blue and yellow make green. Negativity will breed darkness, while light will always break through it.

You are what you 'think' yourself to be, always. You can be a villain, or thief if that is your choosing, but you will have to live with its cost. You please yourself.

No man will ever be perfect in this life – for the whole of his life. This just cannot be. To know all things he must experience all things, before he can know what he chooses, before he can choose what he is, or know his calling.

Just for today, understand that you create your reality with the thoughts you hold and the intentions behind them. It is never too late to alter direction. It is never too late to audit the life that you are making. You are a work in transition and in progress.

(I am I) How can you live a happy life when half of it is kept secretly locked away? To know yourself and to love yourself, you must believe in the whole entity that is you. (I am I)

247

♦♦♦

I am the living voice of the God mind, of Source...

The voice that is you is the accumulation of the knowledge you have gained in this lifetime.

(I am I) Yet you are not just a separate and individual being. You are like a thread in a tapestry. You must understand that your thread is a single part of a greater whole. Without your thread the whole would be incomplete. There would be a blemish. All that is you – all of you – combines to make that of me. (I am I)

Your knowledge, even until today, is but a framework for the being that is you. It has given you lessons and strength and direction.

(I am I) It has formed the identity by which you are known. (I am I)

The life that you know will serve you as it always has, but it will not always complete the missing links that you carry inside. It will not help you become happy and whole because it is a half-life; a half-existence. It caters for the physical alone.

Yet you are not alone and you are not just a physical being. The physical will decay and fall away through the destruction of time. You – that part of you that feels and knows life – are an energy being first and foremost. You are an energy being, living life through the vehicle that is your body. You are connected to the whole of the Earth by your consciousness – by your own soul.

When you live life as though you are separate, you limit all that is you. When you wake up to the truth of your real time connection, you are plugging yourself back into the whole. You are allowing yourself to be whole.

Just for today, understand that the voice you use is also that which connects to the rest of the world.

(I am I) Be yourself, but be your whole, true self. Be open and honest. Be your highest truth and be the very person that only you are. (I am I)

248
❖ ❖ ❖

I must not be afraid of change.

(I am I) The essence of change is growth. The essence of remaining still is stagnation and then decay. To change is to grow, to move, to live. The essence of life is movement. (I am I)

The evolution of life requires change. When we take a look back through time, definite bands of change are evident. Even during the span of one human life, change must play the part that it does. To stand still when all about is altering is an impossibility, and even when it is achieved it places limitations upon the individual who then falls out of sync with life.

Just for today, embrace all changes that fall into your path. They may feel uncomfortable, so ask with your thoughts for this feeling to be recycled. Ask that you be helped to move forward for the highest good. When you see others who are stuck, ask silently that they receive the help they need also. You have the blessing of your creator to move forward with love – in the now.

249

❖❖❖

I must walk through life with my eyes wide open.

To see reality as it occurs is not always as natural as we would think. Social conditioning and individual mood and emotion can colour a lot of what appears to be true.

The truth is always the truth. It is the bottom line. It is that which scrutiny cannot sway.

When we walk through life, it is surprising how much we can miss. When you have your eyes wide open you see not only what is ahead, but also what lies behind, beneath and to the side of the picture. You can see life from all angles and nothing will slip past unnoticed. You have your feet on the ground and you know exactly the place you are at.

Just for today, take the time to notice the whole picture that is taking place. Are you pulling in the right direction, or does the key to the solution lie elsewhere? Send your thoughts out to God, to the universal consciousness, that you may see the truth as it is. Ask for life's truest colours!

250

♦♦♦

I must do the utmost to speak up for myself at all times.

The problem with speaking the truth is that we are not always in control of the outcome of the other party's response. We cannot control how life will act and react with the contribution we must make.

(I am I) The voice that you have is your connection to the rest of the world. It is how you make yourself heard and understood. It is the way you communicate the input that is yours to share with the world outside yourself. (I am I)

When you do not communicate your truth, others do not have the true picture that concerns you. When you leave lots of blanks they will be filled with illusion or misjudgements. For others to know you and know exactly how you feel, they must know your side of the picture. When you think you are misunderstood, then ask yourself why. When you feel put upon, then again ask yourself why. Do you correctly portray your likes or dislikes? Do others know the boundaries that apply, or are you over-accommodating? When you expect too much of yourself, how can others know that they do too?

Just for today, keep your cards positioned correctly on your table. Take this opportunity to regain your sense of self and what is realistically fair. When you do more than you should, too often, you allow others to do less than they ought. You must speak your mind with kindness, with understanding and with love, to allow life to shuffle and realign.

251

❖ ❖ ❖

I must help God, Source, keep the peace.

You are the eyes and ears of the creator. You are present in the now, so you are a prime candidate to relay what is present and required, what must stop, must engage or must continue.

To be able to be fully operational in the now, your mind must be uncluttered, unbiased, and completely present. It needs to be free of clutter from the past and free of illusional turmoil.

To work with the universe, with source, is a gift, but it is also part of the function that mankind was created to perform, as the relater of what it is to be alive. You are all you should be, but the best you can be, must be worked to achieve. This can be as hard or as easy as you make it.

Only you are placed uniquely as the witness of the now that connects with your life. You can see clearly what has occurred and what is needed still.

Just for today, from your own vantage point, realize the uniqueness of your position. When the present moment requires something that is lacking, you can use your thoughts to ask for it. You are the keeper of time. You link creation, through Source, to the present.

252

❖ ❖ ❖

I must endeavor to keep in touch with old friends.

During the course of life it is normal to make friends and strong attachments.

The chapters in the life of a person will alter from one year to the next. Events will change and so will the people you connect/integrate with. You will outgrow life as a child outgrows clothes. This is natural. It is equally natural to keep in touch with links from the past. You share an affinity of the times shared together – not your whole life.

Just for today, when you think of an old friend, look them up. There is probably a need to reach back to familiar ground and to people. There might even be an opportunity to bring the friendship forward into the future – the time you now live and enjoy.

253

❖ ❖ ❖

I always work within the boundaries of good conduct.

Man made the laws of man, but they are also the guidelines of peace and order.

Man is free to do all that he wishes, but he must also consider the implications of his actions and their effect on other people. Law and order are necessary to prevent chaos. The natural world must exist in its own state of order and man is a part of that world. This is the necessity of life.

Just for today, be aware of the way in which you operate and also of how others operate, relate and integrate with you.

(I am I) I too must remember the promises I made when I gave man freedom of choice. I too must stand by those original laws – regardless. (I am I)

254
❖❖❖

I must be open and honest in my words and my actions.

This is not always as straightforward and easy as it would seem.

The thoughts we carry, the things we hear and the images we see do not always tell us the truth of the moment. We tend to fill in the gaps too smoothly and automatically. Sometimes we do not even realize that we have.

How many times have you jumped to a wrong conclusion? How many times have you said the wrong thing, or had the wrong end of the stick? To get things wrong is human nature, but it should teach us to learn to be more careful.

The art of communication is as varied as there are blades of grass in a field. Few people are able to get all things right 100 per cent of the time, and knowing this, must not make us complacent, but more aware instead.

Just for today, be as open and honest in your words and actions as you can possibly be. This will help others to connect to the truth through you. When you always remain honest, you will leave room for little misunderstanding or illusion to take hold. You will be a brick in the times that are necessary.

255

❖❖❖

I must be open and honest with myself.

We can fool other people and deflect their attention, but we can never hide the truth from ourselves.

I have had to learn to be open about life and also about the things I feel and think. When you try to keep the peace, it is easy to take too much of life upon yourself, upon your own shoulders, but when this happens, you merely rob others of the truths, good and bad, that they need to complete the picture that they should have.

Life – good and bad – must always happen to everyone. This is how we learn to shift and change – in stages. You must not shield another because you fear the outcome, nor take necessary action or decisions on their behalf – without their knowledge or consent.

Just for today, be as focused as you can with all that occurs in your own court. Take the time to hear others out and voice your opinions without excess words or hidden meaning, if not at that very moment, then later on when the timing is better. Do all that you can to remain balanced and at peace, but when fluctuations occur, let them be recycled, without any more input from you. Ask for the right words to be given at the right time, for you to pass on.

256

❖❖❖

I must hand my troubles back to God, to Source, to help me through.

Asking for help is not the same as expecting all the work to be done for you, without your own input or assistance.

To ask for help is to indeed ask for assistance. To ask for assistance means that you need another pair of hands to help lighten the load, or another head to discuss things with for another point of view, or for a completely new breath of fresh air. When you hand things up to God, to Source, you are asking for assistance. You are saying you need outside help in the form that will apply to your highest good, to reach the best outcome available at this time. You are opening a new avenue to allow for maneuver and growth.

When you let God, Source, take care of you, you open your options to the aid of the universe. You make yourself available for any kind of help that can come to your rescue or aid. This is the way things should be. This is the way man was intended to behave. When we hold onto our problems and try to deal with them alone, we mistakenly send out signs and signals that we wish to hold tightly to the situation at hand, and that we actually want to do it all ourselves. Yet the opposite is more often true. We look high and low for what we need, and try our best to sort through what life and people present along our journeys path. We believe we have no option but to do what we always have done.

Just for today, ask again for the help that you require. Know that when you hand your problems out for assistance, help is surely what you will then receive. Keep your mind and options open, until you know exactly which direction is best to go. You indeed must do the legwork, but the universe will always assist.

257

❖❖❖

I must be able to get cross without losing my self-control, or my edge.

(I am I) The trouble with man is that he has largely lost his control of his self. Even when he believes that he has got control, it will often transpire that he has not. He must loosen his grip or completely let go, to regain what through time has been lost, and for many this will be almost impossible. (I am I)

The lessons that man learns first teach control of the body and of the self. His next years are spent controlling the life that he interacts with. Even in friendship or family units, man must learn to place himself where he is most likely to achieve his desires or their highest outcome.

Yet to retain self-control, the opposite is more often necessary. When we want something we push and pull hard to get it. We move high water and mountains if we think that the action will help us. We have become far too focused as a species on the physical aspect of living life.

Just for today, when life does not go in the direction that you desire or think it should, don't get cross, let go. The reason you are cross, is that life and specifically other people, will not listen. Again you are asked to let go and to move with the flow. The universe knows what you must achieve and it knows the way best for you to travel. Let it guide you, even though it might not fit into your current, well laid plans. When you feel uptight or wobbly inside, let go of your anger, worry, stress, irritation, and return to a place of inner peace. Only then can you live as you should and keep hold and control of the self.

258

❖❖❖

I must have the patience of a saint at all times.

How does a saint behave?

The picture that we have of a saint is built up through time and story and need, but all those who have once walked this Earth were people as we know people to be. They ate and they slept. They were children who then grew up, but not before doing all the things children do. They had to live and experience the trials of their times, in the same manner as people today. Life was as it was for them as your life is what it is for you.

Through the course of their life they will have performed or fulfilled some outstanding deeds, and these options are still available to you.

Just for today, as you walk through this life, look about you. Look for the little things that you could do to ease the burden of someone else's load. When you get into the habit of going beyond the norm, you will gradually open your life to its own unique style. You will live as much for the well-being of others as you presently do for your own.

259

❖❖❖

I will have all that I need when I need it.

The universe existed long before man became a part of it. It will last much longer than the current species that is man. The universe can take care of itself and it will take care of man too if he can let it.

The law of cause and effect overrules anything that man can put into place. Nature must itself bide by its boundaries. The laws of the people must also operate within the laws of cause and effect. This is the ruling of life.

The world that you know you might sometimes take for granted. Many things come 'as natural' or 'easy'. Could it be any other way when you have known this for all of your life? Because things operate naturally, like a well-practiced play, into action and place, it is only natural again that without effort or thought, all you need must also fall into place.

(I am I) The universe knows every step you have trod and every path you have ever undertaken. It knows your mistakes and misconducts, as well as your triumphs and goals. You are part

of a greater whole, so how could it be anyway else? (I am I)

Just for today, recognize that you are not alone. Know that you are being cared and catered for. That someone else is looking out for your needs. Sometimes what we think we need seems not forthcoming, but really when we open our eyes and look in another direction, the thing we needed most was there all along. We only had to alter gaze to know or find it.

260

❖ ❖ ❖

I must be able to share my inner most thoughts easily with God, with Source, and in turn will I receive answers.

(I am I) Man cries out in sadness and pain, but how can I reach him to help him when he does not even believe that I can? He does not even acknowledge my existence?

Man is a single part of a greater whole. He is a little portion of me. The consciousness that is his is mine too; only he has the power to use it – over me, through free will. (I am I)

The thoughts that man thinks, he believes to be just his own. He thinks that no one else can hear them. He thinks he has the right to say and do and be whatever he wants within his own mind, but he does not understand the reality. All that he thinks, he will eventually become, because with his thoughts he programs his reality. His thoughts are like shouts that connect to the whole. The thoughts that he has are heard by his guardian and God. How could this be otherwise? How could his connection work any other way? He is a part of the consciousness that is God or Source. And God is the life that he lives.

Just for today, understand the connection that is yours to take care of. Love the life that is yours to love and live. No one will hold against you any thing that you have done, as a parent could have nothing but love, for his child. From this day forth know who you are and be pleased you can make a new start. Every day that comes is yours to fulfil and uphold with the best of the best that is you.

261

❖❖❖

I must be able to be honest with myself.

(I am I) Traditionally man is honest with very few —least of all with his own inner self. He is split many ways over many different things. To remember his essence is to remember his birthright, and it is this that will help him be whole. (I am I)

The nature of man is to struggle through his life to conform to that which he thinks that he must. Yet how can he be the best of himself, when he has no idea of the truth?

Man is born of his father and mother. They made him as one of their own, but their parents also grew them too, and so it goes back down the line. The bodies that we see are only a shadow of the people we are deep inside. We are all individual, because we are totally separate entities, who come together to experience the connection of this life on a physical plain.

Because we are individual we all have different wants and

needs at different levels and times. We are all moving forward in the Earth's evolution.

Just for today, recognize that even though we are connected through family, love and friendship, we are also individual beings, with individual needs and abilities. The world in which you function is unique to you alone. You must be honest and open to allow yourself the flow of life that is yours to live.

262

❖❖❖

I live my life along with God and the universe.

The name that you have was chosen by your elders to be your tag of identity. The name called God is also a form of knowing identity.

(I am I) If I was not known as God, what other name would I be known as? Would that name also have a stigma attached to it? The very word God conjures up many thoughts and emotions in mankind. What other name must I call myself to give man the courage to love me and know I exist? My name is just my tag of identity. Would you hold it against me? (I am I)

Just for today, understand that you really do live your life along with God, Allah, Krishna, Shiiva, Mohammed, Buddha, or any other name by which the God head is recognized. The label, tag, name being used is irrelevant. The point is that man could not exist at all if he were not a living being – connected to the living being, body and consciousness that is Gods. Without God there would be no life and that is simply all there is to it.

263

◆ ◆ ◆

I always live in the light of love and happiness.

The thoughts that you hold program your emotions. What you think and what you believe are what you are and what you will then become.

The thoughts that will harm must be recognized and recycled. They will drain your light until you are tired and drawn. They keep your head in turmoil as you allow them to wander to places that are no longer necessary. They take you into the darkness of illusion, doubt and depression. Man can be the worst judge of his own inner turmoil. He can keep it going forever if he wishes, until he reaches the need to stop. He alone can pull himself together. He alone must clear the thoughts that cause him pain and harm. He must remember he has the right to choose at all times.

To stay in the light is to remain fully alert in the time pocket and moment you are experiencing. When you are able to do this, the truth is always what is. There can be no halfway point, or room for illusion to exist.

Just for today, reach your true state of mindful attention. The thoughts that you have will be none other than those that are appropriate. You will now experience the full impact of the moment you are in. You are creating, the way you were always supposed to, with the creative life force of Earth planet itself.

264

❖ ❖ ❖

I must realize my own connection between the life I live and the wider world itself.

The connection that is yours is your life.

Every person is unique by his experiences, his weaknesses, strengths and knowledge. Just as there can never be two snowflakes completely alike, so it is with man. His basic structure of skin and bones is the same, but from there he is individually unique in every way.

The connection that is yours has been forged since your birth, but it is always open to be changed or updated. You are a work in progress that cannot be sealed until you leave this life and even then you will be in transition to the next place and phase of your journey.

Just for today, take a look at your life from the outside in. Notice who you really are and the face you portray to the world. Then take a look at your hopes and dreams. Are they up to the image that you want? Are you happy and fulfilled, or does life seem to dodge the expectations you harbor? Sit quietly and empty your inner space. Keep your back straight, your eyes closed, your arms and legs uncrossed and send your thoughts out to the God mind, to Source. Ask that you may be shown what you need to see or know for the highest good. Whatever you are shown will be the information you most need at this time. Take it with love from the universe.

265

❖❖❖

I must realize the power of the thoughts that I think and the things that I do.

Thoughts are alive. They go from one point to the next faster than m an can move any part of his functioning body.

No instrument yet exists to measure the force and speed of thoughts that man generates. It is only now being accepted in the scientific community, that conscious energy is the underlying force that binds the whole of the Earth planet as one. Thought is energy in motion and whatever is capable of independent movement is alive.

The thoughts of man are responsible for all that is visible in the human world today. He alone holds the key to his demise or his higher evolution. God cannot rescue him; man must rescue himself by his own mental growth and awareness that will then choose to reconnect to the God consciousness. Man will choose to return home of his own accord, not out of force, but because he will understand that this is where he always was. He will understand that through time he merely forgot his roots and his heritage.

The thoughts of man create his reality. He is not a random ball that is bounced through obstacles in a game, nor are his future and choices already written. He does this for himself with every thought he thinks, in every way, every day that he lives. The time has come for him to wake up to this reality. He is responsible for the day he is in and what he chooses to do with it. Past mistakes can be turned around, not always with ease, but definitely one step and one choice at a time.

Just for today, realize the power that is you. Know that you cannot ever be disconnected from the whole, even in bodily death. Know that you take up where you left off, in this life and the next. Know that you have the power to put the past to a much higher use, as you look back and take what you've learnt. Send your thoughts up to God for your highest good to shine through. All that is yours is waiting to come. All that will come will be for the good.

266

❖❖❖

I must keep my connection to the light pure and true.

The light of the world shines brightly within us all, but it is easily obscured by the influences of life that we subject ourselves too.

A baby is born of innocence, regardless of the parents' history and background. Its light is pure and unaffected by its surroundings. Along the early course of life the light of little children will remain bright. They are on a quest for knowledge and experience. They are not responsible for their actions until they can differentiate between good and bad, right and wrong, for themselves. When children grow up, their light can begin to dull, as they move away from the dreams and visions they once had, and become integrated into the necessities and realities of physical survival and existence. Society intimates their original thoughts were wrong, so they begin to conform to the rhythm of the many.

We are each capable of living a life that is balanced and fair.

We live in a time that is geared for abundance and growth, but as we climb the ladder of success we must see that it is not at the cost of another, and that we only take what is necessary for a healthy, happy life, and that metaphorically we give back just as much, and perhaps even more, than we have used. There are many versions of life – all as good as one another. Every avenue we can imagine is at our fingertips to explore. All we must do is lead a good life, so we can be proud of who we were and what we have done when it is over and we must return home.

Just for today, live up to your highest expectation of yourself Be proud to own the person that you are and don't let the past put you off. You are in charge of the soul essence of the being you really are – so shine, as you rightfully should.

267

❖❖❖

I must realize that mistakes happen.

The mistakes of the past are gone. This day is unwritten and clean. It waits for the input that you will give it. It needs the direction and the meaning that you will apply through your birthright and gift of free will.

Man's biggest fear is that he might be discovered for the fraud that he feels that he is.

He tries his best to better himself, to keep his life in order and to be all that he should, but his past keeps pulling him back. He feels caught up in the motion of what he has done. He is too scared to go forward, in case his past catches up and he cannot let go, because he must be in control of the all that he is. Man is caught rock solid by his own illusion. He himself is the jailor that he fears.

Just for today, let go of that control. Let life come and go as it will. When you alter the rules that used to apply, it will take time for life and things to change too. You begin the alterations from within by your choices, and like a ripple it will gradually work out. People will be the last to see the new you, because for a while they will search for the old. They will be used to the way you were, so it will upset their own life a bit too. Mistakes of the past are built of wrong choices which now you choose to correct. The past was then, and this is the now. Do you really want to drag it forever along with you? When you are really sincere the universe will know, and when you ask for its help it will give it. Ask for the past to be recycled as much as possible. Face all that comes along one step at a time, and realize that the true way forward is beckoning.

268
❖❖❖

I must listen to the smallest voice.

(I am I) My connection to man is so natural to him that often it remains overlooked. His energies combine with mine as easily as he breathes air into his lungs. It requires no practice or thought – only recognition. (I am I)

This life is a chance to leave your mark on history. It is an opportunity to grow and to correct the imbalances and wrongs that exist all around.

This life must be used for its highest purpose, intention and potential.

This life is no rehearsal. It really matters how we live and the knock on effect of our presence, our intervention and intention.

The role of man is the lead role in the story he unfolds of his life. All other people make his character possible, and this is true also in reverse.

Just for today, let the loudest voice in your head be quiet and still. Take a step back and watch as if looking on. Notice the role you have cast for yourself and the part you are expected to play. The smallest voice is your true guiding one.

(I am I) This is your connection to me. At no time would I ever hurt you or another in life. I would not lead you to harm. The truth is the link that I reach you by, and this time is your souls purpose to own. (I am I)

269
❖❖❖

I must be confident in the ability of God.

The Earth existed long before man came along. Man has an important part in its evolution, but the Earth will still survive long after mankind has gone.

The role of man is important, but a far greater role is for God.

Man is a creator, but a greater creator is God.

Man knows many things, but a far greater knowledge has God.

Man can make life, but God is the all life that is.

Just for today, have confidence in the knowledge that you are simply part of a much greater whole. The role you play is important, but as a single link in a larger chain. Be pleased that the weight of the world does not rest on your shoulders alone. Be confident in the role you have asked to play, but have more in the role that is God's.

270
❖❖❖

I must be at one with God, with Source...

(I am I) The life that you live, you live only through me. The life that is mine is experienced in part, individually through each one of you. (I am I)

Just for today, live your life as though it were the most precious gift you have ever had. Take it, love it, experience it and express it.

271

♦ ♦ ♦

I must believe what I am told by God...

Who speaks the truth?

(I am I) I do. (I am I)

The truth is the real story of life that has happened since the time of the birth of Big Bang. To date man has a good idea of what really occurred, but he can never know it all. He was not there to witness it happen.

The truth that is God's is the real truth, but it must depend on man's ability to interpret and to decipher it well. Man cannot know what he does not yet understand. Many things, even today, even with his highest intelligence, fall outside his present sphere of comprehension. Man is still on the voyage of discovery and growth. How far he will go must depend on his openness of mind and his ability to differentiate between the truths he will find and his illusion.

The truth will always stand up to scrutiny. The truth will always be there under your nose, and you will wonder why you had not noticed it before. The truth is the truth – no matter what.

Just for today, notice the truths that fall into your path of vision. Take nothing for granted and everything as possible. Listen to the smallest thought that plops into your mind and follow it through. Once you begin, the universe will realize you are making a connection and it will then help you all that it can.

272

❖❖❖

I must be able to feel the truth.

Man is brought up to know the difference between the rights and wrongs he is taught, but he can also recognize these differences with a feeling. This is an ability that he rarely consciously uses, but nearly always subconsciously feels or hears.

Many people can feel when another is lying. They can feel the change in vibration of live conscious energy, because its flow becomes altered. When a person speaks the truth his energy verifies the fact. Again, just by a feeling, you can tell. Those who work on an energy level finely tune into this ability, but it is a tool that is available to all.

The more you recognize a sense, the more you can learn to use it, the finer and stronger it will grow and become.

Just for today, listen to your inner self. When you feel balanced and at peace, then all is as it should be. When you feel uncomfortable on some level, or when something within does not seem to sit as you know it should, then look for the reason. Send your thoughts upstairs and ask for illusion and negativity to be recycled. Ask for the truth to pull forward and for your inners sense of self to return to peace. Learn to tune in to these feelings as often as you can – to work on ever higher levels with Source, with God.

273

❖ ❖ ❖

I must hand my thoughts over to God, that I may be relieved of my turmoil.

Man does not yet understand the influences of his thought, his mood, or his emotion.

(I am I) The truth is that he does not try to know. (I am I)

Millions of thought combinations pass through his brain every day. Some he latches onto without knowing and others seemingly come and go at random. The ones he holds on to are the ones that continue to keep his illusion of past and future alive. He replays themes over and over again – often without any conscious effort behind them.

The only time that exists in reality is the present moment, as one long now... All other time frames stem from this one. When man allows his thoughts to overrule his commandment of the moment, he robs himself of fully living in the present that exists. He allows his energy to drain slowly away until he is left tired and drawn. How can he live with the zest of planet life when he unconsciously keeps running, away from it?

Just for today, when your mind wanders, bring it back to the present. When you get caught up in someone else's illusion, step out of it as soon as you can. Life is for the living, so consciously keep hold of the time frame you are in. As soon as you recognize your pattern, hand all that you no longer need back to God mind, to Source.

(I am I) I will bring you safely back to peace. (I am I)

274

◆ ◆ ◆

I must recycle the disagreements I encounter.

(I am I) Life is both positive and negative in nature. No man can be totally immune from either vibration. Good and bad will at some time touch all. (I am I)

Nature needs storms to clear the air. It moves heat and energy from one level to another whenever necessary, for the good of the planet. Sometimes this is productive and sometimes it seems not, but the Earth could not survive easily without them.

(I am I. The Earth was born because of a storm, a storm of proportion that man will never know. (I am I)

Just for today, when you encounter a storm of emotional turbulence, recycle it. Whether it is yours or another's, recycle it the same. The God mind knows exactly how to quell it and you are simply opening the doors to let it happen. When we hold our tongue at times we should not, then we add to the drama itself. When we scream and shout at times we should keep still, then again we add to the drama. When we agree with another, just to keep peace, we also add to the drama. Only God can pull some things back together, but to do this, man must let God, let Source come on in.

275

❖❖❖

I must help Source help me...

(I am I) I am always with man, but until he learns to know my presence, he will always imagine he is alone. (I am I)

Man has the freedom to use his life, yet he feels alone and cut off from the world. He thinks he just uses Earth's surface, but does not know that he influences its wellbeing.

Man lives on the body of God and connects to it through all that he is. To speak with God is simply to think. Nothing is lost on the way.

Man is the present link in a long line of descendants. He has helpers and teachers, relatives and guides – all working together with love. They do this because they know life is sacred. It is important we get the 'now' right.

Just for today, let God and the divine kingdom come into your life. Allow the help and the love to come through. You are a physical link in a world made of energy. The Earth is the sum of us all.

(I am I) I have been waiting for man to understand this. I have tried many times and many ways. This is the truth that exists. This is the true heritage of man. (I am I)

276

❖❖❖

I must be prepared to share the knowledge that is given to me by God, by Source, by the universal life force that is.

The knowledge of man is passed down through generations. This has always been the case. It is how he learns and grows, but man can only know as much as there is available to know, as much as his intelligence can grasp. He can only know what himself or others have discovered along the way. Yet this is not all there is to know – it is only what is known at the present time.

When you open your life out to God, to the Source, you open your channel to greater knowing. You not only plug into the knowledge of the forefathers, but to higher wisdom and philosophy too. Your ability is only hampered only by your willingness to believe. When you know the truth, have been shown the truth and live the truth, you know it with all of your being.

Just for today, believe in the knowledge that comes to you. You are ready. You can feel the truth. Have faith in your ability to acquire the truth and share it with all that you can. You are the voice of the truth.

277

❖ ❖ ❖

I must believe.

(I am I) You are real. You believe that to be true. Your life is real. You believe in that too. I am real, yet you find that hard to swallow. I am the all that is. Yet I have to prove my existence. (I am I)

Man can never be greater than God, yet it is God that has to prove his existence.

Man is a small living part of God, yet he does not believe God's existence.

Man has faith in other men, yet he finds it difficult to have faith in his God.

Man becomes all that he needs from the goodness of God, yet he does not believe his existence.

Just for today, believe that God is for real. This is the truth that has been right by your side since the day of your birth and beyond. All that you are has first been your choice, but now you can go forward with love. Open your life, your heart and your mind to the truth that has always been here.

278

❖❖❖

I may not always be popular when I speak my mind.

The world consists of many facets, each one as valid and important as the next.

The truth that is yours is just a part of what's true: the part that is true to you. Yet there are many truths that make up a whole, and all must be heard at some time.

When you speak your truth you are stating how you see things to be. This is true at this moment in time, until you update it through further knowledge, practice and understanding. A truth that is told is often a stepping stone for you or for somebody else. No truth is final, because life is subject to growth and alteration. If the truth were rock solid, how could it evolve? The truth is your truth to share.

Just for today, when you have a truth to be shared, then do it with love and with ease. Be honest and open about what you feel, so it can be used as a tool to move forward.

279

◆◆◆

I may live as I choose to live.

No way is the only right way.

(I am I. If one way was right that would mean another was wrong. Then how could man learn who he is? How could he know who he is not? All aspects of life are correct because the needs of man's life vary greatly. (I am I)

The world is in constant evolution and growth. It strives higher and harder to reach its own best, as a tree will not stop until it's reached its full growth.

Just for today, recognize that you have the right to live as you choose, but so has the rest of the world. You live by the choices you make and sometimes you pay the price too. Send your thoughts up to God, to Source, for your highest good, to find the best way for you to move forward.

280

◆◆◆

I must allow others to live as they choose.

We have clear ideas as to what we deem acceptable and what we think is not.

Families live together and conform to the chosen guidelines that they always have. Friends become friends, because somewhere along the line they are the same also.

But all people are not the same. There are distinct differences that tell them apart and it is these that can rub us up the wrong way.

Just for today, when another makes you feel irritated or cross, allow them the right to be free. Give them some space and recycle the negativity that is surfacing. The universe needs all of us just the way we are. Ask that love and light may be at your side and go forward in your day, as you should.

281
❖❖❖

I must not dwell on things that do not occur in the manner I have been told that they would.

The thoughts and plans that we have are simply illusion until they have been brought to life's fruition by action. Thought is energy in motion. It is raw creative possibility and power. At the stage of thought anything is possible, and when we are prone to allow those thoughts to run away, we can build up a picture that would be impossible to achieve.

Another fact to remember is that when we think, we do so alone. The act is void of outside information, input or interference. Thoughts take the form of idealism. In an ideal world, all things are possible, but in reality, life can find it hard to compete.

Just for today, notice how thought interacts with real life. When we take one step at a time towards our goal, a goal that we still have a lifetime to achieve, all things are possible. When someone or something falls short of expectation, don't bury your head in your hand, but instead know the reasons of why. Perhaps it was meant for a later date, or did the idea take all it should have into balanced consideration? All things that are meant to occur will do so in their own true time frame and proportion. Just let go and move forward to the truth of the day you are in. Ask for left over disappointment to be recycled and that peace return again in its place.

282

❖❖❖

I must not always believe everything that others may say.

Man operates within his own world, on his own plane of possibility and illusion. Very few have the ability to live completely in the truth of the reality of the moment.

Many people have their own view of life and with it their own envelope of truth. To them the rules that normally govern good conduct and interaction are different. They are tailor-made to fit the image they have of themselves and again the image they believe that others have of them. To people such as these the world is a place that is threatening. They continuously try to prove they are something they are not. They have little self-esteem even though their behaviour would have you believe the exact opposite.

Just for today, when someone has trouble fitting into the truth, send them the power to do so. Ask God mind, Source, to make its connection and ask for illusion to disappear too. Ask that this person may be given all he needs for his divine highest good. Ask that he be given the help to go forward in the true light of the all that is. The truth of the matter is that by doing this you have achieved more for this person than years of the usual response. You have taken the trouble to tell the truth to help that waits patiently to come in.

283

❖❖❖

I must be vigilant with my thoughts.

Thoughts are not the private property of man, but are instead his connection to the consciousness of the greater living world.

The mind has been used to free wandering. Even when it knows it should not. Curbing of thought can be a difficult habit to acquire, especially when we are quiet, relaxed and contemplating, or at times we are worried or stressed.

Just for today, remember that thought is energy in motion. The smallest of thoughts we think are just as important as the more conscious episodes. When you realize you have been off spinning in another direction, bring yourself gently but firmly back to present. Send your thoughts up to God, to Source, and ask that they can be recycled and brought to peace. For at least a few minutes make a deliberate effort to keep your mind on the present moment at had.

284

❖ ❖ ❖

I must be able to accept all that life has to offer.

Life is neither good nor bad. It is just what it is. It is life.

The life that you know will alter everyday. The vibration of events will dictate the urgency of those events as we live.

(I am I) The troubles that arise must be dealt with. The high will always follow the low. Happiness is a natural state, but that too will come and go, because no thing remains always the same. Life is continuously turning. The best you can do is always enough. No one will ever expect more. When you look at each day as a tribute to life, the pace will flow by itself. (I am I)

Just for today, let life lead you in the direction it chooses.

(I am I) The problem is just to let go. (I am I)

You are a single part of a greater whole, and the trouble with that is you cannot control the whole thing. Just be yourself and allow life to come and go as it will. All you need do is keep up.

285

❖ ❖ ❖

I must be able to make amendments to my work when necessary.

No man is perfect in this life.

Man must do his best at all times, but his best is only as good as the ability he has. There is always room for growth and improvement, otherwise he would not still be here.

When man needs help the universe will always provide it, when necessary, but first he must ask and then he must recognize its approach when it comes. Next man must be prepared to listen and accept the help that is offered and when he does, it becomes a part of his growth.

Just for today, take the help that is offered. You have a good mind of your own, but sometimes someone else has a tool that will help you tweak your life further forward. Send your thoughts out to God and ask that you may recognize the wisdom when it arrives.

286

❖ ❖ ❖

I must recognize when I have done enough.

There is always a point of time when any more action is overkill. The trick is to know when to stop.

Nature itself will only go so far until it has reached its peak. The trouble with man is that he has forgotten to turn back and look at how far he has come. He is like a train that has missed its stop.

Just for today, take a look at the life you come into contact with. Have any of these avenues grown tired and thin? Is it time to let go or to help another see that the project is complete? When you feel there is no more to be achieved send your thoughts out to the universe and ask for it to be taken over. Ask that you move forward for the highest good, that the old can fall away and that you be given the tools you now need.

287

❖ ❖ ❖

I must be at one.

To not be at one is to be fearful, stressed and troubled. You work against the currents of life that could help.

To be at one is to be totally effective and at peace with the moment and events you are experiencing. To be at one is to be open and relaxed in your approach to life. You are completely aware of the world that surrounds you and you know exactly the part that you play. You know what to do when it is necessary to do it, and you are open to the influences that come to help. You are not afraid to be angry, in proportion to the scale of event, but you can let life ebb and flow as it will because you are one with it all.

Just for today, know you are totally at one with the universe.

You are at peace and in love with your world. People will do what they always do, but you will cope in a fine balanced way.

(I am I) You are at one with me. (I am I)

288

❖❖❖

I must be happy with the life that I have.

The life that is yours is your current existence. You are here to enjoy its experience in its entirety.

It is a common occurrence of man that he believes he must only reach to the end of his days before he can find the better place that awaits him. He believes he is at the mercy of life and its influences and problems. Many have lost their live zest for living. They live as though treading through water, they go through the motions, but arrive nowhere.

The truth is somewhat different. Life is continuous. There is no death, therefore there is also no birth, only rebirth. Life is a series of transitions from this world to the next and back again, many times. Each life is a unique experience. Man may alter gender, class and nationality. Man will experience all there is to experience on the body of the Earth. That is his heritage and his choice. No person will enter into any life under duress. It is always by freedom of choice.

Just for today, know that you have chosen to live life on Earth at this time. Take a look at your life, at its heartaches and consequent lessons. Look at the positives that have come despite the negatives experienced. Look at your life in terms of the choices you have made – the good ones and those you'd now term mistakes. Look to see if you are pleased with your lot. If not, then look to see how you could better it. Look to see the part you played to get where you are. You make your own rules and your own decisions. No one is to blame for the experiences you have known. They too were simply locked into their life and looking for their way, as you yourself are still doing. Send your thoughts to the God mind and ask to be taken forward for your divine highest good. Silently ask the same for those who have hurt or angered you in present or past. Ask that happiness be here now for you all.

289

❖❖❖

I must not worry.

The human mind has learnt to worry. This is because we let it. The mind simply does what we allow it to do, and until we learn we can curb it, it will continue.

Just for today, recognize the patterns of your thinking. When you operate from worry mode, then you are living in the dark cloak of fear. Fear of not being able or good enough; fear of others and what they might say and what they might think. Fear of life in any form is very simply fear. Ask God mind, Source, to bring you back to peace. Ask that all illusion be recycled and that the truth of the issue be revealed. You are in control of your own state of mind; so don't let it roam alone in the darkness.

290

❖❖❖

I must channel my thoughts and fears at all times.

The thoughts that are produced are living waves of energy. Man gives them power with his intensity and intent. Man chooses his subject matter and then thinks it forward into action.

(I am I) Man is linked into Source – always. At no time is he ever alone or disconnected. He just believed that to be. The power of this link is not yet fully grasped by anyone yet upon this Earth. (I am 1)

The reality of the life that is yours is all the product of thought. You have designed your own life.

Just for today, recognize that your negative thinking holds just as much clout as the positive, but know that the negative has no place in the time of your now. Let it go. You have sense and intelligence. You know exactly what you are doing and where you need to be heading. You have at your disposal all the tools that can take you there. Ask Source to help you. Let go of your fear and channel your best into now.

291

◆◆◆

I must be better than my best.

Your best is just an illusion. There is no limit to the best man can be. He has the force of the universe at his disposal. He is live creation in force.

No one is telling you that you must be better than your best – instead you must only recognize that you are. You can surpass your wildest dreams just by working to do so. The reality of ability of course must apply and man must be realistic in his endeavours, but the truth remains that when we apply ourselves safely and wholeheartedly to life, there is no end to the things we can achieve.

Man must have faith in life. He must also have faith in himself. When he learns something properly and overcomes his fear, then there is nothing that cannot be achieved. The life of every person is as important as the next. All possibilities are open to all people all of the time.

Just for today, recognize that you are better than you believe yourself to be. You are the creative living consciousness of God, of Source. You have the whole of your life to enjoy it. The truth of your divine being is waiting for you to recognize yourself. Allow this knowledge to filter through – now.

292

❖ ❖ ❖

I must not feel guilty at things I cannot manage to do.

You feel guilty because you have set your sights unrealistically. Either you or someone else has been too rigid in your expectation of the thing that you have guilt about.

Life flows. It can never be static. We can set ourselves a target, but when we occasionally miss it, then so be it. It is pointless throwing energy and undue thought and distress at what we cannot change or undue.

Just for today, when life takes charge, don't worry. Go with its flow and know you can catch up at your earliest convenience. When you worry, you get stressed: and when you are stressed, you are grouchy and everyone will feel the effects. Talk to God, to Source, and ask that you can come back to peace and tension and pressure be recycled. You will complete your tasks when the time is better suited to do so.

293

❖ ❖ ❖

I must be aware of the feelings of others.

The body of God is the Earth that we live upon and it is through this that we all interconnect.

Man is an individual spirit on his own individual journey. He also touches the life of others as he mingles and communicates through normal daily grind and activity.

The thoughts that he has, portray his immediate needs; his physical make-up is much the same as others'; his hopes and desires are his own; his past is unique and his future unwritten and his feelings and emotions reflect his inner state being.

Man has been on a long journey that began many eons ago. With each new Earth life his soul learns more than he knows.

(I am I) I will verify this. (I am I)

Each new day is a day to be lived in the manner that best suits his life, but along the span of that life, distinct patterns and behaviours emerge.

(I am I) It is not for man to be afraid of this knowledge, but more that he lives a good life. He will not be perfect – at least, not until he knows the importance of his time on Earth. Then he must change, because he will choose to do this of his own free choice and will. He will understand the pointless things he does and will instead find the truths that are his. I will be there by his side when he does. (I am I)

Just for today, be aware of the feelings of others. Recognize that they are souls the same as yourself, just looking to find how they fit into this life. You are lucky, because you know the higher truth, but perhaps they do not know the same. Ask silently that they may be guided in the manner of their divine highest good.

294

◆ ◆ ◆

I must be lenient with the misunderstandings of those around me.

Every soul is on a journey of progression. The level he has reached will be where he is now, but it will vary from person to person.

The world is made up of many people with varied characters and intellects, varied pasts and desires. Each is uniquely different because of the life that he knows.

The levels of the soul's progression must vary also according to individual people. No soul can ever regress. At the level of spirit it can never unlearn what it knows, but along the course of an earthly life it can become stuck, so it will not progress any further until the time it is freed and then can.

Just for today, recognize that not every soul will be as advanced as you. Some will be more and others less. Their needs and intelligence will be different. When you get mad, don't scream and shout, explain what you need them to know. Give them your time, not your negative vibrations and look for the positive instead.

295

❖❖❖

I must keep my divine house in order.

The nature of man is to place others before him self, but he must take care of his divine energy too. He must primarily keep his own life in balance, or he may miss something important that he needs.

The base of his own life must be solid and strong, his health must be kept and his personal space uncluttered. He must be up to the minute in all his affairs and he should have all that he needs to survive. His mind must be centred on the time of his now and his past must be at peace in his thoughts. He must realize his worth and the lessons he has gained and the strengths that are part of him too. He must be able to be every aspect of himself and at all times be open and free. He must take care of his commitments and his daily needs, but he must also remember his heritage.

(I am I) He must remember he is part of me. (I am I)

Man's internal mind is also his house. It matters how he lives within, what he does with his thoughts, what he chooses to believe, where he lets his private mind roam. What he does with his intentions, how he manages his feelings, his emotions, his wants and his needs, how he uses his time and the life that he lives, have equal importance and merit. Man is never alone, so there is nothing he can hide from the connection that is his to the world. From this moment on the past is done and gone, but the present is where his mind ought to be.

Just for today, as you go about your business, remember that all should be balanced. Every aspect of a well balanced life will create a well balanced whole. The balance of mind is most important of all, because it is from here that all reality stems. Your outside behaviour is but a mirrored reflection of what is occurring within, and what is within is your connection and offering that you're channelling to God.

296

❖❖❖

I must recognize the help of God, of Source, when it has already been given.

Man lives in a physical world and all things about him reflect that.

Before man recognizes his connection to the planet he believes himself alone and meandering through life. He believes he is at the mercy of life rather than at the creative helm of it.

Man really is immortal. This is fact, not fiction, and never before has there been so much information available to tell us all so. The world is demanding that we wake up, that we realize the potential that lies within our own grasp. Every person everywhere can make a difference, no matter how large or small, somehow, to something. This also is fact.

(I am I) The more man awakes, the more he will return to the truth of his own inner self. The more he can let go, the richer and happier he must become. For the whole of man's life I have been trying to wake him. The pull of matter is strong. Even at

the times I've been close, his mind would convince him it was wrong. How can I begin to portray the joy of having him back? How is it possible to reunite with the self that never was lost? Yet to all intents and purposes, man was lost. He imagined himself all alone. Yet now he is realizing the truth, and all that was his, is still with him, within him. He must realize one bit at a time. The myth of his God and his soul everlasting is not myth at all, but the truth. He is finally on his journey back home. (I am I)

Just for today, know you are being guided. Know that you are loved and cared for – no matter what. Take the pressure off those who love you, because the love of the planet is with you. It's the love of the God Source itself.

297

❖❖❖

I must be flexible.

Nothing is built to go on forever – except the conscious intelligence and power of life.

The whole of the world is vibration. It is energy and light and chemical mass.

Man is a part of the world. He is here to experience life.

Just for today, recognize that all things are able to change. Things change all the time, yet nothing really changes at all. Life itself must keep all things in check – by cause and effect and natural balance. Know that all you must do will actually be done, by you in the full face of time –tomorrow!

298

❖❖❖

I must be myself.

The life that you own – is yours to live.

The many different spans of life that each soul will experience are individual, and specifically chosen, for its own highest purpose and progression. Each soul will further every aspect of self expression, growth and knowledge before completing what it birthed to achieve.

The span of one life in Earth time feels long, but it's only a flash in the time scale of spirit. It is not long enough for the soul that is yours to express and expand, to contribute, to aid and create.

Just for today, live! Express and experience your soul time. Discover something new about you... Ask God that your perception of time passing can be slowed to its minimum; that you'll be able to do whatever you wish, as opportunities present or become available. Let this day be devoted in the higher soul sense – to your essence of expression, love and laughter.

299

❖ ❖ ❖

I must remain balanced through the shocks that life sometimes delivers.

No man is immune from the turmoil of life.

The richest person has problems; the poorest person has problems. Problems are problems – no matter what their subject or size. Problems highlight areas that need attention. They are often the effect of matters overlooked or forgotten, unattended or ignored far too long.

Just for today, take any problems that arise in your stride. They are alert signals, no matter how big, and once dealt with correctly, they will not return. Send your thoughts up to God and ask for assistance, that whatever necessary be recycled and easily resolved. Keep your mind on the moment and keep watch for the solution; you must remain on alert till it appears. A shock is a problem that hits you like a house. Again you must come back to an inner state of peace and balance, and an innocent frame mind, to be able to quickly pass through it.

300

❖ ❖ ❖

I must be the eyes and ears of the now.

You are waking up to the reality of life, but before you did you lived mainly in the future or the past. Your mind was rarely in the present where it tries to be now.

The life of man is changing. The vibrations of the planet are changing too, largely because of the changes in man. As he wakes up, so the planet will also change gear.

It is important that man lets go of illusion. He must let go of his past and step into the now. Every effort is given to help him achieve this. He is trying to go forward in life.

You are more fortunate than most, because you are aware of the changes and growth, but many are not and perhaps will never be in this present lifetime.

Just for today, recognize that you are firmly rooted in the now. You have your finger on the pulse of your life. Your eyes are wide open and your ears hear very well. You are being asked to look out for problem areas. You are being asked to direct help with your own mind to those areas that need some assistance. Send your thoughts out to God when someone needs help and ask for that connection to be strong.

301
❖❖❖

I place the need of others above myself...

(I am I) The importance of man is equal. There is no order of importance. All people are the same to the planet. They sustain their needs from it. They should return all they can back to it. (I am I)

You have your life under control. You know what needs fixing, so you fix it. You know what needs attention, so you tend to it.

You obtain what you need when you need it and you live your life as you please.

This is how it should be. You are here to obtain that experience. Yet others are meant to do the same. They too are experiencing life. They too should be engaged in the flow, yet at times the opposite is true.

People's lives will ebb and flow at different times on different levels. This is the law of individuality and karma. This is cause and effect in operation. In an ideal world life would be good for everyone, every day, but the truth is the opposite in reality. Life moves up and down daily and so must its influence.

Just for today, when you see someone lagging, reach back with your hand and pull them up. The path they are on might be heavy and hard, and for someone to take notice might be all that they need. Remember, you are just a connection, so send your thoughts out to the God mind, to Source. Request the best help for their highest good, then let go and let it come in.

302
❖❖❖

I must be bright and cheery in the face of darkness.

Darkness is the result of trouble, turmoil or stress.

The forces of light and dark affect everyone everyday. They are responsible for man's shifting moods and emotions. These in turn affect his thoughts, his feelings and his life.

Man has complete charge of his mind. When he can recognize the pattern that has hold of his day, he can opt to change it at will. He can learn to recycle the darker moods that dog him to lift himself higher above them. This is not always an easy feat, but with patience and practice it can become a more common behaviour.

No man's life can be harmony and light always, but the day is his to enjoy as he can. The tools he needs to help him are available always. He has only to recognize their existence.

Just for today, when events or moods pull you down, push them away and be happy. Recycle the things that you really don't want and take a step up in the process. A better frame of mind will achieve far more and will even attract to him the positive.

303
❖❖❖

I must do all that I can to keep my own life in order, and God will help me with the rest.

The ability of action and non-action lies in the hands of each man himself. He is must do whatever legwork becomes necessary to achieve his goals and aims, for he is the one who is physical.

Man knows the state of his affairs. He knows the ins and outs of his whole life so far. He knows where he's been, the ideas he's had, the routes he's taken and those he's yet to follow through. Sometimes his efforts may appear to go wrong, but he went down the path he chose for a good reason. He had to properly know the ins and outs of what would and wouldn't work, to then know where he now has to go.

The life that you live is put together step-by-step like a puzzle, where each piece must fit or at least touch together.

Just for today, take the inspirations that you get and work swiftly to follow them through. Some may seem to take you astray, but then you are free to take the next step. You can only know what is right when you definitely know what is not. Send your thoughts out to God mind, to Source, and ask for your path to be free to open up. Ask for the help that is yours, and allow it to follow through as it will.

304

❖❖❖

I must be honest about the way I think and feel always.

Your thoughts are the keys to your kingdom. You can fool other people from time to time, but you can never tell a half-truth to yourself. You know the score of how you think and feel, exactly.

The things you believe to be true, usually are unless you are prone to illusion, and illusion serves no purpose at all. You know yourself better than any other person could. If you cannot be honest with yourself in terms of what you think or want, then how can you expect other people to?

(I am I) Thoughts are the signals you send out to the world. They reflect your own worth and your sense of wellbeing. They

depict the direction you intend to go and also your connection to your surroundings. They relate your relationship to others and to life. Their instructions program life, they are receptors for that yet to come through. (I am I)

Just for today, be aware of the thoughts you send out and also those you that choose to hold onto. Your thoughts are your own, but they are also the help that is given to you as inspiration and advice straight from Source. Remain open and honest and notice when something you need comes to mind.

305

❖❖❖

I sometimes stand back so that others can do what they must.

You are the creator of your reality, but so too are others of theirs. You know what you must do and how, but you are just one piece of the world. It takes all people everywhere to make up the whole that is life.

Just for today, let go of the helm. Allow others to play their part too. You are working towards the good of this life, so let go to go further than you could by yourself. The good of the world is a part of us all, so have faith in the knowledge that you are a part of the team.

306

❖ ❖ ❖

I must take the time to have fun.

Life is a serious business, but it is also full of uplift and laughter.

The life of a child is worry and carefree. It is filled with wonder and discovery, happiness and challenge. Rules and regulations will also apply, but each day is a day to be lived. This is the way it should be.

When man grows up, responsibility is his weight. He must protect against all of his fears. He lives life by his watch and the pressures he feels and often he forgets about fun. He forgets that the world is a wonder-filled place. He looks out, but his eyes do not see. He is locked in the prison of his internal strife and waits endlessly for someone to notice.

Just for today, be aware that you have placed yourself within your barriers and walls. The door is not locked against you; instead you just need to walk through. Life is the same as it ever was and what you make of it is entirely your choice. Take the opportunity to laugh whenever it occurs and have fun at the times that you can.

307

❖ ❖ ❖

I should gain happiness from my own choices and decisions.

All that you are, you have chosen at some time, but today are you happy or not?

The truth of your choices might not always be pretty, but you chose them because you believed that they would be. You hoped you would be happier; you hoped that your wants and needs would be met. Yet many times this was not always so.

Just for today, realize your lows as well as your highs and notice where further adjustment is needed. You should be pleased that nothing is final, that instead, you are a work still in progress. The life you are living is yours to be written, so make corrections wherever you must, choose and re-choose when you feel that you need to. You are a part of the whole of this world, and its help is available now.

308

❖ ❖ ❖

I must check before I offer my advice.

The help that is needed might not always be yours to freely give.

People are on their own unique pathway. Sometimes we can clearly see where adjustments should be made, but unless people are open to receive, your help or advice will go unnoticed. The timing might not yet be right. There will be times that we are destined to walk a little further, before we can find the things that we need.

Just for today, before you offer your advice as assistance, check that it is actually needed. To be too upfront at the wrong time will be seen as interference instead. Send your thoughts up to God, to Source, and ask for that help to occur in the right way, at the right time and level. Ask that all concerned be given what's required for the highest outcome and good. Know now deep inside that you have done what you should. You have made the connection that will put all things straight, and your friend has their pride still intact.

309
❖❖❖

I must not take another's anger too personally.

(I am I) The necessity for anger is more necessary than we know, but it must be relevant and in correct proportion to the problem. (I am I)

The need to express your truth is equal to both positive and negative. To recognize our own boundaries, or the boundaries of life, is as important as teaching the truth. Too many people do not know how or when to stop. When a limit has been reached you must show it, for if you don't, how can anyone know?

Just for today, recognize that others have their limits too. They may just be letting off steam, or they may have a good valid point. The thing to remember is to learn the truth behind their outburst and to put it right if you can.

Send your thoughts out to the God mind, to Source, for assistance and help, that all surplus negative energy be recycled. Let communication and truth be the order to come in, and let the matter conclude as it should.

310

❖❖❖

I understand that I write the script for my own life with the choice of thoughts and actions that I take.

No person is responsible for who you are, even if you clearly think they have been.

Man and life will interact with your life on all levels, but your choice of action, non-action or reaction is up to you. You always have control of yourself.

At no time can you be immune from the things that will happen. The best people must still interact – with the planet they are part of.

Just for today, know that this day is unwritten. You alone can steer its course. You have yourself in your own hands, but your mind is connected to the Source of all that is.

311

❖❖❖

Others will always be as they choose – for that is their choice.

The life of another is their prime responsibility. They must take care of their life as their charge.

Man likes to mix and spend his free time with others, but sometimes this can be hard. Each life will dictate its own priorities and his attention must be applied to them all.

No man can live by his choice alone, and sometimes life nudges him further along. He must allow his behaviour to fit in accordingly. He must stay completely in tune.

Just for today, when others make an excuse, be supportive and understand why. They have their own life and commitments to adhere to. They must meet the demands that arise.

312

❖❖❖

I must talk to let others know the way I think.

Man has the gift of communication, but how effectively he puts it to use is another matter.

The freedom of thought and speech enjoyed by many today has not come about easily. Throughout the ages men and women have lost their lives fighting for such. The powerful rich felt threatened, the poor felt unheard, the church used it to place fear in men, and the uneducated were vulnerable, all through the words of man. And so it continues today.

Today man has free speech. In many countries he can think and say what he will. Yet communication is just as difficult, as we work to make ourselves understood. It seems it is not the words used that matter, but the emotion, intention and force which lie behind them. Words depend also on the understanding and mood of the recipient.

Conversation must pass two modes of comprehension before successfully being taken on board.

Just for today, recycle all excess positive and negative energy, both inside your own field and the environment you are in. Keep yourself open and focused on the moment at hand. When you have something to say, say it. Keep it honest and simple. When you do not
understand what is being relayed to you, ask for it to be repeated until the time that you do. Thoughts matter, so when they are put into words make sure that everyone has the complete picture.

313
❖❖❖

I must think before I talk.

Thoughts we have do not always speak truth.

Man is often subject to illusion or misunderstanding, yet he takes his next step according to his understanding of the moment. The reality he believes he sees is not always the truth itself.

Just for today, make sure that you know the whole picture before you give your opinion. Many hours of trouble can be spared when we take a little more care. Send your thoughts to the God mind and ask that truth be your guide. Let illusion fall away and take the time that is necessary to think things through a little further.

314

❖❖❖

I must treasure each day as though it is my last.

The day you are in can never come again. Take it and use it as you should.

Tomorrow is an illusion based upon the thoughts of today. Yesterday is no more. It has left its mark on time. Today is the time frame that matters, the time that man must get right. The rest of the future is born from this day, so it matters how it is spent.

Just for today, be vigilant with your time. Use this day to its fullest potential and tie up loose ends that are trailing.

315

❖❖❖

I must be able to be myself.

Each person is individual. The identity that he holds is unique.

Every person fits somewhere on the surface of the planet.

*(I am I) Even though he might not think of himself as important.
(I am I)*

Because no two people can be completely the same, the life man chooses becomes tailored to fit. He is primarily an energy conductor for Earth. It is important he is comfortable with being himself. He must be at one with his life and his surroundings. He must be happy in the life that he leads.

To be happy, is to allow positive energy to flow and stem from you easily. To be negative is to be a disruptive force. The effect will be like a turbulent storm that upsets life's subtle balance wherever it flows. A negative force is no good to the Earth. The force that it needs now is positive.

Just for today, be open, be honest, be yourself. Let no thing and no one pull you down. Have faith in your character, your ability and your talent. Know you are needed because of all that you are. You are a unique link in the connection of the God mind.

316

❖❖❖

I must not interfere when I get the help I have asked for.

Man has a crazy habit of always wanting to be in control, even when he does not know what he's doing.

We ask for help and then know better ourselves. We want to learn, but run before we are able. We need a hand, but become agitated when it is not fast enough.

Just for today, let life dictate its pace. When you need help, have faith that it will be delivered. When you are asked to help, do so if it is appropriate, but if not, be honest and let it come from the source that it should. Use your thoughts to direct it as necessary. You are the link to the reality of now.

317

❖❖❖

I must take the time to connect properly with others.

How often have you been misunderstood? How often do you misunderstand yourself?

Life is an orchestration of movement and connection. Each person must play his part until he connects or interconnects with another. Man must take his energy, use that energy and move it freely, until he changes his task to the next. No matter how menial, each job must be worked on until it's complete. This is the law of cause of effect. An unfinished task is a still open end, and that has no purpose at all.

The Earth needs man to connect. Each time a task is complete, man makes a positive connection. Each time he passes a piece of information, correctly, at the right time, man makes a positive connection. When man helps others understand or he does so himself, he makes a positive connection.

By being late, we fail to connect. By being over eager we loose some of our fizz. Timing is more important than we know, this must be perfect for all things in life to properly fit.

Just for today, notice how many connections you naturally make, because each time you do, you help life to flow. When life runs smoothly, all its connections fit, but when trouble and chaos are brewing, then someone's connection is amiss. At the first sign of trouble send your thoughts out to God and ask for help to connect. Ask that the unnecessary can be removed and a positive be put into place.

318

❖❖❖

I must try to keep my head clear of whirring thoughts.

Interference blocks energy waves.

Man is an energy transmitter, receiver and manipulator. He lives his life as he must, but on an invisible level he works on behalf of the planet.

Thoughts produce positive or negative energy charges that are then put to life by man's action. When he lives in turmoil, his vibrations are equally disruptive. He produces nervous energy that puts others in his surroundings on edge. Nervous energy disrupts any positive charge in its vicinity.

Just for today, be mindful of the thoughts you think and transmit. The Earth needs your balance to help life flow. The power of mind is stronger than you realize.

319

◆◆◆

I must live according to reality.

(I am I) Reality is the truth of the moment, the cold hard facts as they exist. Man lives more by illusion than the truth of the real time. He operates from within the version of life that he wishes to see, rather than from the reality that really exists. The world at this time is not always a pretty place. Fighting and poverty are rife. The difference in class still very much exists although often it is shrouded by man. (I am I)

The world needs us all to wake up. It is necessary for our own evolution. What occurs in the news affects us all, even though we might not realize how it could. The truth that we know is only the tip of the iceberg. To see the whole thing would be frightening. The world is in need of restoration and man must play his part.

The world is out of balance and the behaviour of man holds the key. He is out of sync with his own life and so transmits chaotic vibrations.

Just for today, remove all of life's frills and see the true picture, but don't paint it too dark with fear and negativity either. This is not the end, but neither is it the beginning. Just the now that is left in between. We ask help from God. We take all we need from the planet. Only now it is necessary to get our own act into balance, for it is here that what we do matters.

320
❖❖❖

I must be honest and open in all that I am involved.

The world needs stability. It needs things that will never change. When man puts himself forward to say, 'follow me', he must be true to the mould he has chosen.

When something is stable it can be relied on to always be the same. That's why it is important to be vigilant in the everyday things that you do. The ordinary tasks may seem mundane, but they create a good base in our life. When these things remain done, they free up the time we have left.

Just for today, be open and honest with yourself. Be the anchor that others can turn to when they are confused or worn out. There is more to life than being a high flyer. It's the little man who helps the world run.

321

❖❖❖

I must help life along when it gets stuck.

Life requires constant movement, or it is prone to quickly stagnate.

The law of cause and effect is responsible for much that we know; yet man is often oblivious to its truth.

Man rushes through life without a thought to the part that he plays in the scheme of existence. It's not that he should stop and worry about life, but more that he should take greater care and responsibility for the planet he interacts with.

Through the lessons of history we see clearly the march that man has made with the progression of time, yet today he seems more stuck than ever. He has come to the peak of much that he does, and now he is bored and restless. The only avenue left is the one to extremes; all that he does, he does to excess and extreme.

Just for today, take a look around you and notice how very lucky you are. You have all you ever wanted and even more than you dreamed. Take a step back and enjoy being exactly where you are. The biggest obstacles in your life are the ones you have placed in your mind. Let them go and recognize the truth as it really is.

322

❖❖❖

I must be nice so that others will be more inclined to help me when I need help.

The day you are in is a blank, unwritten page. There is no reason to be any other than your best.

Look about you. How many people do you get along with? How many people do you consider get easily along with you?

The door of communication has never been more accessible. People from all over the world can talk to each other without the normal problems of culture, language, boundaries and class. When you are nice, people are generally nice in return.

Just for today, realize that being nice will take you much further than being a grouch. When you get angry you do so alone. You close all your shutters and you push people away. When you see someone else that obviously needs help, send out your thoughts for the truth. Ask for the connection they need of the Earth and ask for their peace to shine through.

323

❖❖❖

I must be able to recognize unexpected gifts I receive from God.

(I am I) To recognize the gifts you obtain, you must think that I do really exist. (I am I)

There is nothing man has that first was not given. The normality of life is also a gift: The truth of forgiveness, the truth of free will, the truth you are loved for yourself, the chance of a new start with each day that comes, the reality of your connection to God and how God is connected to you.

Just for today, do not think only in terms of physical gain, but more in terms of life's attributes itself.
The gifts of the creator are always apparent. You do not earn them. They are yours anyhow.

324

❖❖❖

I must be prepared to accept the gifts of God.

When have you had rubbish just thrown upon you? When was your name used to curse? When have you been told you don't really exist? When was the right time to pray?

You create the life that you have, but the life that is God's is hard. He has no control over the species of man, he must wait until man trusts the fact he even exists.

He gave man free will to move through his life, but man has forgotten his truth. God waits in the wing for man to return to his heritage of line.

Just for today, take note of how man treats the Earth. Every being is responsible for his own little world and in turn its connection to Earth. You do not have to follow the pack. Use your own mind. Make your own stand and do what you know to be right. Recognize you remain part of God.

325

❖❖❖

I must understand that I cannot always remove the hurt that another has to experience.

(I am I) Life has many levels and man passes through each of them in turn before he can move onto the next. The time he will spend on each is determined by his own strength of character and ability. It is determined by his soul's own progression and the life that his karma must live. No man is destined to remain statically in one place. The world holds the same possibilities for all. The power of the universe is available to all. No boundaries exist except in man's mind. This is the truth of God's will. (I am I)

No man can skip a level. He must complete each one in turn, under his own effort and steam. He will overcome problems and some might be hard, but they cannot be removed except by his own skill and judgement.

Just for today, recognize that the pains of life are periods of growth. We can ease someone's pain, but we cannot remove it entirely. Only they can do this. Try to understand and help them find the solution they need, but never remove their ability to work through the situation. The power of life is with us all, we just need to connect and go with it.

326

❖ ❖ ❖

I must be able to help only when my help is warranted.

The first instinct of man is to help those that need it, but this is not always correct.

There are people that never do anything they should, because they have learnt that others always will. They are expert at knowing the exact way to ask, so that others will help them instead. This is fine up to a point, but when their tasks become the burdens of another, the balance is not how it should be. Both parties are wrong to shuffle the load, because the universe placed it as it ought to be.

Just for today, before you jump with both feet, check that your input is warranted. The lessons behind much that we see can run deeper than at first might be apparent. When you see someone struggling you can give them your hand, but be careful they don't shift the load. Send your thoughts up to God that all will be balanced. Ask that things may be as they should. If you are meant to help, then so be it, but beware of the lessons that lay hidden.

327

❖ ❖ ❖

I must do the best that I can with the day that I am in.

Everyday is a good day until man deems it otherwise.

The time that we have ticks evenly away and often it slips quickly by. How many hours do we really enjoy and how many days do we waste?

The potential of time usage is unlimited. How man spends it is completely his choice, but how often does he consciously try to use it for the best that he can?

Just for today, try to do something good – anything, just one thing. When you do the same each day, your efforts will build up. The positive energy you will generate will come back to you magnified.

328
❖❖❖

I must not take on board the mood swings of another.

Look about you. Do you know of a reason that you should not be happy?

Life is relatively even. It slips by uniformly each day. Nothing much alters until the time that it does, and even then it returns as it was. When others around us feel the need to get cross, when their mood swings unsettle the flow, you make the choice of whether you join with them or not. You choose to twin with them, or to help them move forward as best as you can.

The mood swings of another is their own affair, unless you yourself are the cause, but even then you can stay calm and move through the turbulence easily, just by drawing your energy field back into yourself. Every person operates from within his own centre of energy. Ordinarily we can touch and interact comfortably, but when another is moody his sparks can be felt as they fly all over the place, and, just like a fire, they will ignite anything that gets in the way; but you don't have to let them, you can shield yourself until it's over.

Just for today, allow yourself to be as small as a grain of sand. Imagine you can draw your energy field inside, and then draw it back down to your feet. The turmoil of others will fly safely past and you will be protected somewhat from its sting. Send your thoughts to the God mind and ask that the turmoil be recycled. Ask that your colleague be returned to peace. Ask for the situation to be brought to a successful close and that balance remains in its place.

329

❖❖❖

I must act on my instincts at the time they are received.

(I am I) The instinctive nature of man has been built up over the course of many lives. (I am I)

Instinct is different to impulse. The instinct of all living things is inborn.

Man must be in tune with his own self, and his now is the only place where this happens. He must have removed his turmoil and barriers, and he must be fully present and functional in the time he is experiencing. The truth of the moment is always the bottom line, and because he is balanced he will notice the slightest fluctuation in his thoughts, feelings and emotions. He will be in tune with the highest good of the universe.

Just for today, have the confidence to listen to your instincts. You are in tune with your life and surroundings. You have the tools of life at your fingertips. All you must do now is notice.

330

❖❖❖

I must keep my day moving forward in constant progression.

Life is not written in stone. It is not a chore and neither is it to be lived as such.

It is normal to have routine and commitments, but it is also normal to have days that are slow or bursting with excess energy. Nature must live at its own natural pace.

Man moves too fast too often. He must listen to the rhythm of his body, of his life and its surroundings. When he overreaches in one respect, he must compensate in another. He must keep his own self in peak condition and balance.

Just for today, take the time you need to bring your life back into order. When you go too slow you must catch up on things that call for you to do so. When you have been burning yourself out, slow down. Take time to connect with reality and touch base. Life will always move forward, it must, but you are simply one piece of the larger picture, not the whole thing. Send your thoughts out to the universe and ask for the balance your life needs to bring it back to optimum performance.

331
❖❖❖

I must ask Source to help me through the day I am in.

Man is a single part of a greater, working whole.

(I am I) I am the body you live upon. I am the hand that feeds and caters for your needs. I am the God who knows you better than you know yourself. I have witnessed all that you are, through this life and previous ones. I know your fears and your dreams. I hold nothing against you, but offer you all. I am the one who can help you – in your now. Always. (I am I)

Just for today, recognize the connection of unlimited potential and love. Know that by knowing your true heritage you allow the creative force to weald its power through you. You walk hand in hand with the source of all life itself.

332
❖❖❖

I must believe that I am worthy to ask for help from God.

(I am I) You think yourself unworthy because you know the truth of your past, but you have forgotten the promise of my love. You have listened to the fear of man, before trusting the love

of your true protector and life force. If you deem yourself unworthy, then you call me unworthy also. How can you be what I am not when you are connected to me through life? Do you think you can do anything to sever my link? (I am I)

How can a lung full of air be disconnected from the breath of life? It cannot. How can the life of a man be disconnected from the planet? It cannot. All you are and all you have been is not the same as all you will ever be. You are a life in progress, in transition. You grow and change from day to day. You are living the reality of your creation.

Just for today, know that you are infinitely linked to the all that is. There is no other option. To think yourself to be anything else is illusion. You are worthy of assistance and love, because of that connection. Again there is no alternative. Ask with your thoughts for the help that you need, because without that request, it cannot be forthcoming. You have to ask with free will. You have to talk to the God mind itself.

333

❖❖❖

I must be able to stick to the boundaries of good conduct.

The law of nature must follow its guidelines, as man must follow his too.

(I am I) The laws of physics govern the universe. The Earth must operate the same. Man is part of the Earth and he lives by its cause and effect. (I am I)

The boundaries of interactive behaviour fall within the law of cause and effect. The thoughts and actions produced will determine the future to come. Man can do as he pleases, but nothing can be hidden or overlooked. The history of man's life is recorded within his own energy field. It is the record of the person he is.

Just for today, be the best version of the self that you can aspire to be. Use this day to set your life straight. The past is over, but you can alter your now. You can choose how you would rather it be. You are the jury you will judge yourself by. Have faith that you can live your life right.

334
❖❖❖

I must believe the progress that I have made.

Material progress is easy to measure; the eyes of man can see it all, but personal and spiritual growth is not always so visible. It is easy to think you are dreaming. It is easy to let it all slip by.

You are the product of your past intention, before you woke up to the truth. To trust in the truth, is to live it as you learn. To trust in your progress, is to know how far you have come. The road of truth will not let you down. You must trust in the guidance of God.

Just for today, know you are being led along every step that you take. The route you take will be personally tailored to fit. You must believe in the process of life.

335

❖❖❖

I must believe compliments that are handed to me.

The need to compliment someone comes from a feeling that manifests as a positive thought. We have a need to share what we are thinking at that precise moment, so the words burst forth and without hesitation we share our thoughts.

The need to pass on a compliment is spontaneous. Often we have little conscious intention in the matter. We say what we think, because at that moment we are unguarded and open. We speak our truth and feel glad that we did. The energy we needed to share was successfully delivered.

(I am I) Words are energy manifest. They reach their target the moment they are uttered and their effect can linger for years. (I am I)

Just for today, when someone passes you a compliment, accept it. Even though you might not be sure it is genuine, accept it, because on some level it probably is. To make light of it is to rebuke it. To dismiss it is even more negative. Just accept their words and let the matter be. Always.

336

❖ ❖ ❖

I must not fear – even when situations around me become fearful or violent.

Fear is the negative response to the moment.

Thought is energy in motion. Word and action are energy manifest. All form of communication and action is energy that is being born. All energy is either positive or negative in nature. There is no other alternative.

When the Earth was born a war existed between positive and negative atoms. As they collided, they either multiplied or cancelled each other out. As energy slowed its vibration, it formed itself into matter. The Earth was formed in this way.

A war of energy particles has been waging ever since. This is the nature of life.

Man is the latest link in a long chain of evolution. He is the creative force of God manifest. Each person is a small chink of the whole. He is responsible for his interactions within his world.

A war of positive and negative still wages, through man's interaction with his life on the planet. He is connected to the planet by design. All he does will also affect the planet – by design once again. The energy he manifests through his lifetime is the energy that is transmitted back and forth through the whole to God, to God's body that is really the Earth. The war between positive and negative is primarily fought through the choices, intentions and actions of man.

Just for today, when you are fearful and the world about you is raging, don't add fuel to the fire with your fear. You feed the event and make it more intense. How can you cancel out the negative with even more negative? Instead send your thoughts to the God mind and request the help that you need. You are a source for the positive to connect to the now. You are its guidance point. Ask that you can be as small as a grain of sand, and that you be protected until the storm is over. At the deepest level, the struggles and fights of man are manifestation of the age-old war of positive and negative cancelling each other out. Man is the key that will determine which of these forces will prevail.

337

❖❖❖

I must have and behave with the innocence of a child.

The mind and intentions of children have the ability to be neutral. They are open vessels for the forces of life to seep through.

The ability to remain neutral will help you remain unfazed through the turmoil that life sends your way. You will deal with it with ease. Nothing will get you down and nothing will hamper your growth. You will be at one and in sync with the world.

Just for today, allow yourself to be like a child. Take life as it flows and deal with it with ease. Be confident in the being you are.

338

❖❖❖

I am.

(I am I) I am. These words are my words. They are possible through all that you can see. All that is now, I am. Free will and the ability of knowledge were inherent in man that he could know himself. That he could know and experience the wonders of the world around him. That he could create and express of his own accord. He was given the ability to know beyond the limitations of other animal species. I am manifest in all that surrounds man. I am the Earth that gives man life. I am the thoughts that man chooses to think. I am I. (I am I)

Just for today, understand that whatsoever you do unto yourself, or another, you also do unto God.

God is the life force, without which there would be no life.

(I am I) I am the total of all matter and life of the Earth. I am the all that is and you form one single part. (I am I)

339

❖❖❖

I will.

(I am I) The will of man is individual and small, but when it then becomes the will of many, much can be accomplished. (I am I)

The will of God far exceeds the will of man. God is the highest will of all. Yet still, alone it can do nothing. Free will was given to man. The will of God, no matter how righteous or correct, can do nothing without first the thoughts and desires of man. Even God itself cannot take away what God has given. To do so would render the very nature of free will null and void.

God's will must first be man's will before it can become manifest. Man holds the key to his own destiny. Man is now creator – not God.

God is the total of all, but man is the force that must reach out to God. Man must learn that God is real. There is no life without God, because God is the sum of all life.

Just for today, realize the power of the will that is you. You have the will to succeed. You have the will of creation through the very will that you weald. The final chapter to the book of your life will be totally written by you. Make sure that you will be pleased with the finished product. Make sure you live the life you intend.

340
❖❖❖

I must be resolute in my efforts to be the best possible version of my true self.

All options of life are available to you – daily.

You are the sum of the life you have had, but you are not yet the sum of the all that you possibly can be. You choose your options daily. You create the program by which you then operate and live.

Just for today, do not underestimate your ability. Settle for nothing less than the best you can be. Now is the time that matters, because now is where all time is born. Nothing can prevent you from reaching your highest good. Know that every option is open to you to choose from.

341
❖❖❖

I must be vigilant in my best behaviour and take the world as I find it to be.

Life is not always kind and good, but the truth that you live is the life you have access to right now.

We can be all we want to be in our mind, but the real test comes when we attempt to apply it to reality. Boundaries and problems are things that must be addressed and overcome. When you are careful, you can take life as it comes, but take care not to be pulled down. It is easy to get tangled in a web of confusion, but not when you remain focused on the truth.

Just for today, know that everyone around you is hunting for the key to their own peace of mind too. We are all in the same boat. Try your best to stay above everything that happens, and let the world sort itself out as it will. Send your thoughts over to God and ask for the highest good to shine through. Ask that you can remain focused and at peace until the end of your day.

342

◆ ◆ ◆

I must learn to trust life — even the seemingly bad parts.

Life is not all sweetness and light. Death and decay play their part as they make room for the new, born of the old.

There is good reason that man cannot see his own future before time. If he could, he would never move forward. He would not wish to face the troubles that allow him to grow. He would remain where he was instead, where he might not feel happy but he would feel comfortable in his familiar old role.

When life is particularly good we feel strong and energized. We take on the world as it cares to appear. We are at our peak and this is precisely why we are encouraged to move up a level. We are able to withstand the obstacles that karma dictates must be overcome: the obstacles that will benefit growth.

Just for today, when you feel let down by the world, when people about you are raging, know you are in the dark before the dawn. You are probably bearing witness to the cause and effect of karma. Think that you will be alright –and you will. Sometimes it can be easy to get caught in life's crossfire, but unless you are directly the cause, know you are being protected and helped. Ask that the whole affair be recycled and controlled for its highest good, and that the auric field of all parties be smaller than a grain of sand. You are bearing witness to creation at its highest. You are the creator yourself.

343

❖❖❖

I must heighten my awareness to the help that is at hand.

There is always more to life than what instantly meets the eye.

The eyes see matter. They can only see what is thoroughly solid. They can only see what they have been taught to see by the recognition of the brain.

Yet life operates at many depths, on many levels. There is more invisible movement surrounding man than he can yet understand.

The awareness of man to recognize these influences must be personally learnt. He must teach himself to be open to the experiences that the universe offers. He can, if he chooses, remain as closed as he presently is, but in that case he will only hinder himself. The universe must and will grow around him. It cannot do anything else. It is up to man to open up to the experience.

Just for today, make up your mind. You must choose to be open, happy and receptive, or closed. You call the choice. You have the keys to your own destiny. You throw the dice that you call.

344

❖❖❖

I believe in the truth that exists in the reality of this life.

The truth of man is open to growth, conditioning and persuasion. The truth of the universe is the highest truth of all.

When man fails to open his awareness, the truths that he needs will come forth in louder and harder lessons. The Earth needs every channel it has to be open and fully functional. Where there is blockage, it will send a means to unblock it. Where man is stagnant, he will have cause to change through problems that must be overcome. No man will be left behind in the planets evolution. Not for his own sake, but for the good of the whole.

Just for today, be aware of the lessons that are trying to update you. You are surrounded by love and by light. You are needed for the channel that you are. You are who you are by design, so recognize the truths that are being offered. Deep inside reality is the very thing you need most – to move on. Send your thoughts out to God that you may be open to receive all you should know, now.

345

❖❖❖

I have the light of the world by my side.

The light of the world is God.

God is the matter and consciousness of the planet Earth. Man is a part of Earth.

Man is one small part of the whole.

God is light, so man is light also.

Just for today, recognize that you are a part of a living, greater whole. Go forward in the knowledge that the universe is right with you, protecting you, loving you and urging you on.

346

❖ ❖ ❖

I must be.

(I am I) I am the light of the world. You are a part of me. You are a channel for energy and light. When your channel is fully functional you are a vessel for light to pass through. You are responsible for the smooth functioning of the vessel that is you. When you are closed or cluttered with turmoil, stress and negativity you must work to clear out your space. You cannot fulfil your planetary obligation until you do. Your life will not be able to flow as freely as it should until you do. (I am I)

Just for today, recognize that life is helping you along. Where you are stuck, it will highlight the problem. When a problem arises, realize it is nothing more than something you must deal with to move forward. Ask that you may move through it correctly and know the help you require will be waiting. At all times be your true self, for the self you are is exactly the person you should be. You fill the space that is yours.

347

◆ ◆ ◆

I must live.

(I am I) The life that you have, is given to you by God. You are part of the planet and the planet is part of you. The planet has a conscious mind all of its own. Every form of matter has a part of this. The life that is man has the obligation of being the creative force that must lift the planet to its next stage of evolution. The planet cannot stand still, as man cannot stand still. The whole of life must move and grow, or it will die and stagnate. Man puts the life force back into the living planet. The planet must rely on man to replace what he has used. The planet needs positive vibrations to keep it healthily maintained. (I am I)

Just for today, realize that the creative force must operate through you. You must live – the planet must live. You form your part of the God mind. It can only live through you. The version of life that is you must do all that it needs to do. You are the only one that can fit that post.

You must live so that the planet can know itself in its entirety.

348

◆ ◆ ◆

I am with God.

You are with God, because you cannot be apart from God. You form part of God's body. You are sustained by it. You have life because of it. You are a small part of God, so how could you not be with God?

Just for today, know that you are in tune with your life and its connection to the whole. Know all that will happen, will do so because at some level it is necessary for it to be that way. Don't worry or panic. Don't fret. Let life flow and keep yourself balanced and your behaviour correct. Respond to the moment with the energy that is required, and then let the matter go and move on. You are with God. The flow of creation is operating through you, and as it does, it can cause some surprising twists and turns. Ask that your energy field be as small as it can be and plough through your day as you need to.

349
❖❖❖

I am living the dream.

(I am I) The dream that was mine was to know myself, to know and experience the planet. The dream that was man's was to do the same. The dream that is you is your life. The dream that is man's is to live a happy life, to know people who love him and to love in return: To be the best at what he chooses to be and to do all he wishes to do. (I am I)

Throughout the ages man has dreamed of making his life and his world a much better place. Many gave their lives in search of such things. Even in your own time span battles have been fought and lost and won. The world that you know is derived from the dreams of mankind.

Just for today, stop and look around you. Have you reached

your original goal posts, or are you like many others, too busy to even notice? The dream you live, you do so by choice. The choice to dream is yours by design. Ask the God mind to recycle your illusions. Ask that you can see your truth and recognize how you came to be living the life that you are.

350
❖❖❖

I have nothing to fear anymore.

(I am I) The bible depicts the original sin in the Garden of Eden. The Earth you live upon is that Garden of Eden. The original sin was man's own fear, and because he feared he was closed. He had closed his connection to me. (I am I)

From that point forward, man has lived in his fear. He helped it grow because he felt he was alone, and he has kept it going until this day.

Yet man is not alone and he never has been. He just lost his link to the consciousness of God, of Source. He lost his ability to communicate his thoughts. He has been lost in a life of confusion.

Just for today, know that you have never been alone. All thoughts that you have ever had have all been heard. The only difference now is that you recognize the connection. You recognize the God link in everything. Never again must you fear. Never again need you fear. When you get caught up in momentary madness, recognize it as such and let it go. All you do not really need will be recycled. All you do need will be returned in the most appropriate manner. The Earth that gives you life is the Garden of Eden that was intended to be your paradise.

351

❖❖❖

I have to believe in myself.

To not believe in yourself, is to live in doubt. Doubt creates confusion and that gives rise to fear. To live in fear, is to live under a cloud of darkness and of negative thoughts, and to live like that is to be miserable.

Belief must begin with oneself. To help others believe in you, you must also believe in yourself.

You know how far you have travelled along the route of your life. You know the wars you have waged. You know those you lost and the many you have won. You know the limitations that have been overcome, and you know the obstacles you still have to face.

Just for today, believe in your own ability. You are the master of your destiny. You have trained your whole life long for that privilege. The universe is right at your feet. Believe in the best that is you.

352

❖ ❖ ❖

I must loosen the grip of routine in my life.

Life must be allowed to flow as it needs to.

Routine and order are very necessary requirements to keep a well balanced life, but sometimes we are too rigid in their adherence. We can become too routine minded.

Just for today, lighten up a bit. You know what needs to be done and you will still do it, but allow a little interference to break the cycle. Work will always be there, but life will quickly pass you by if you don't connect to it. You are simply altering the order of the day, not cancelling it entirely.

353

❖ ❖ ❖

I must sometimes allow others to make their mistakes.

Life is never as clearly cut as black and white.

In a fairy tale, life can trundle along forever on a sweet note, but there it is pretend. In reality, real life and other people, moods and emotional swings step in. Nothing can be predicted to run exactly as we would like it to, or even as we expect it will.

(I am I) Mistakes happen. They are part and parcel of life. When the mistake is over, many lessons will have been gained by its

experience, often on unseen levels as well as the obvious. Mistakes are meant to be. They clear the air and clear away illusion and false direction. They are the stepping stones of man, not his noose. (I am I)

Just for today, when someone has made a mistake, tell them not to worry. A better option is not far away. To reach it, man must still do the mind work, but that which was destined to be, still is. You can help by sending your thoughts and misgivings to the God mind, to Source. Let all unnecessary baggage be recycled and let the help come in as it ought.

354
❖❖❖

I must take each day and live it as I should.

The day you are in is new and unknown. You have not experienced it yet.

Just for today, let all preconceptions go. The universe knows what you must achieve. It knows everything there is to know about you. Trust that life will work with you to help you, and the day will produce a quality all of its own.

355

❖❖❖

I must take each day and savour it for its own merits.

Man is connected to the Earth. All men are connected the same way.

Your life is one little life compared to the whole of the planet. The part you play may be the lead role to you, but it is still just one tiny speck in the scale of the Earth.

The day you are in is your day to spend, but as you do so, take note. People will go and come and briefly touch your time. This is the way it should be. You may take a wrong turn that will turn out for the better. You may do something unexpected that will be good for another. Whatever the day will bring, it will be unique unto itself.

Then in the evening as you look back upon it, know that it had a merit of its own.

356

❖❖❖

I must ask for God's help before I engage in any uncomfortable situations...

(I am I) Man is interconnected with me always. His life is entwined with mine. All of his thoughts, and also those of the people that interact with him, are known by me. (I am I)

The God mind hears all, but cannot intervene unless directed to do so. When you need help you must say so – in thought. When you don't know what to do for the best, ask for direction in thought to come through. The God mind is forever linked with man's mind. It can be no other way.

Just for today, realize the connection that waits for your direction. All you require will be given, but first you must reach out and recognize that help is already there. Before you embark on any task, always ask for help for the highest good. Ask that negativity and illusion be gone and that truth and love remain. Then go forward with confidence that all things will unfold as they should.

357
❖❖❖

I must face all situations full on, with an open and honest approach.

When man is open he is balanced and receptive. He is neither positive nor negative. He is both.

The wrong way to handle any situation is with an air of preconception. How can you know the experience at hand when you have not had it? You know of similar occasions and their outcome, but not yet this one. Everyday is a new day with its own set of influences. Very rarely are two instances completely identical. There may be similarities, but there will be differences too.

Just for today, keep your mind open and clutter free. Take each individual moment just as it comes and let the influence of the universe come in, as it will.

358
❖❖❖

I must be aware of the illusion that I create for my own existence.

Man is a blank page. Nothing is written that he does not choose for himself.

(I am I) The life of man is not predestined. He must choose for himself every step of the way. He is destined to reach certain mark points to help him along, but the method he takes to reach them is up to him entirely. The life man lives is largely illusion. He can be any character he desires. He builds his whole life around the goals of his choice. He becomes what he believes himself to be. No way is the right way, and similarly no way is wrong. Man just is what he is, until he chooses not to be anymore. No boundaries, guidelines or pressures are placed upon him that he cannot handle. It is man that creates the reality which is his. He is his own master and he also is the creator.

The world of spirit will assist him in his life. The aim is to help him be happy. The purpose of man is to live fully in the now, and when he is happy he can be the energy channel he was designed to be. No life is a waste of a life. What man cannot learn in his physical existence he will learn back at home in the world of spirit. The importance of this life is not always apparent, but the spirit always knows it. Man has free choice of all that he is, but he is never left purposely alone. He is important, because he is physical now. Now is the only time that can change life on Earth. Man is the creator of his now. (I am I)

Just for today, live life as you wish, but be aware that yours is not the only reality that exists. You create your life everyday that you live, and so too does everybody else. You have this life to do all that needs to be done, to the best of your ability. Use it well.

359

❖❖❖

I must allow myself the best that I can find.

The best that you can find does not refer to material and physical property, but to the wellbeing you feel deep down inside.

You can have the best car and the best house. You can have food and clothes and trinkets, but these things do not teach man to be happy. They are feel good factors, but they can also hinder your lifetime growth. When you measure your worth from the things that you gain, you are living in the height of illusion.

The best you can find refers to true peace of mind. To wake up in the morning and be glad that you did. To take the day just as it unfolds and to move along in it with ease, quite flexible in approach to whatever occurs. To love everyone, regardless, and to quickly solve problems at the time of their birth. The best that can be will always be yours, because you are rooted, happy and open. You have the world in your hand. Just for today, settle for nothing but the best. You have an obligation to be happy. You have a life to get creative with.

360

❖❖❖

I must be able to hear and balance out the criticism of others.

Criticism is not meant to wound, but to help.

Man takes to heart the criticism of another, because he feels that he is being hurt, but that need not always be the case. Man can turn criticism on its head and look to see if there is room for improvement instead.

Man is just one life in the scale of the whole, but it takes the combination of all life to make that whole. Man has not just himself to please. He must fit in unity with the life of all life. He must perform his life in the best way that he can.
When others criticize, they do not always intend to wound, but to highlight areas that could be improved upon. Every person is a voice of God; so all are linked and interlinked.

Just for today, don't take the negative to heart and to hurt. Look instead to see if it has any foundation. Look to see where improvement might lead to perfection. When you are faced with the negative comments of others, send your thoughts out to the universe to help. Recycle the feelings that have surfaced and ask for the truth to be visible instead. You are never alone.

When you need a little extra something, the universe will always supply it, but it just might not be in the form that you expect.

361
❖❖❖

I must be prepared to work hard to clear the clutter that is mine.

(I am I) The clutter that man leaves in his path is probably the thing that causes him most harm. Just as clutter in a home traps dust and dirt, the clutter of a person traps and clogs his energy flow. This is a major contributor to illness and depression. Trapped and blocked energy will hold man back for years beyond the point he should have moved on and forward with his life. (I am I)

The clutter of man does not reflect only on his material life and the state of his belongings. Instead we must recognize these as a symbol of his inner mind – his state of mind. The clutter of private property reflects the inability of a person to move on and let go of an outdated past. Yes, memories and attachments are natural, but over attachment to every object symbolizes an inability to operate in the freshness of a new day. With a fortress of clutter around you, how can new experience and intuition possibly win through?

A nut needs a hard shell to protect its delicate kernel, but man does not need the same way. Is it possible to run through a field of rubbish as easily as you can through an open meadow? The answer is no.

Just for today, take note of your surroundings. Take note also of your inner state of mind. Are you able to sit peacefully within your own space, or do thoughts of past events keep coming in; events that bear no significance to now; events that even to themselves were unimportant? Send your thoughts out to God mind, to Source. Ask that all unnecessary thought and clutter be removed from your being. Ask that you can be as small as a grain of sand in you psyche and that you can be fully in tune with the moment at hand. Ask for the help you need to let go of that which you no longer require. Clear your space, inside and out, and notice the change in the way you now feel.

362

❖❖❖

I must be patient with the beliefs of others.

We are all part of the same whole. We are the same. Yet on some levels we are completely different.

(I am I) Every being is born into a body. The willingness to be born is the same for all. Yet everybody is the vehicle of an individual soul, on the journey of progression back to the ultimate - to God. Like on a ladder, each soul must climb the steps, and with each step comes a different living and learning necessity. With each soul comes a different set of requirements that need to be met to clear the stage it is on. No time scale is given. It is the right of each soul in turn to take all the time it will need. No extra points are given for being first or last. The only requirement is to complete the journey in the best possible manner that you can. No soul can regress. It can remain static

and stuck through the whole of its life span, but it can never go back down the ladder of growth. When it cannot grow on Earth, it will do so when it comes home to the spirit world. (I am I)

During the course of a life, man lives and learns at the speed which is right for him. Again no limits are set. The object is to live this life and be happy with it. To love and to experience all that it can. When it lives in sadness and strife, it is stuck. When it needs a nudge, the universe will provide it.

The type of life man chooses for himself is irrelevant. The problems he must face will help him to grow as he overcomes them. The beliefs he acquires are much and the same. They reflect the level of mindful growth he has attained to. He is the master and creator of his now. He can bury his head or he can enjoy his time. The choice has always been his.

Just for today, do not judge anyone at all. Accept them for who and what they are. They are beings of energy and light, just the same as yourself. They may be at a different level of understanding, but they are just trying to live life in the only way they know how. Be your true self at all times and allow your influences to touch. You both may be helping one another.

363

❖❖❖

I must be able to be as busy as I would like, but I must recognize the patterns I am stuck in.

The way you conduct your life is the way you have

programmed yourself to be.

No person made you the way you are. All people are simply being true to themselves. You are who you are, because of your reaction to the experiences and information you received.

The person you are has been programmed since birth. You are all you have chosen or allowed yourself to be. You will also program the person you wish to become, but instead of haphazard influence you will choose to make educated choice.

Everything you do, you do in a pattern. You choose that pattern yourself, depending on the importance you place upon each task. When you wish to change, you will alter the pattern by which you operate. You will conduct your life in a different manner.

Just for today, recognize the outside influences that dictate the pattern you live by. Recognize that nothing is written in stone, and if you feel caught in a trap or a rut, then find out why. Look to see how the pattern might be updated to allow for improvement and spontaneity. Ask the God mind to assist you in making the shift. Recycle all unnecessary illusion and watch for the insights you need.

364
❖❖❖

I must be able to take the negativity of others and turn it around to its positive lesson.

The negative is a signal that all is not well, that someone or something needs to be addressed.

Negative thoughts are destructive. They are miscommunication and misunderstanding at their best. When someone around you is negative it is a sign that they need to be heard and understood. They might have a valuable point. The best-laid plans can grind to a halt when a spanner is thrown in the works.

Just for today, make sure that all sides of the picture are seen and understood. The positive side of negativity is understanding the issue and new growth. When you are unsure of what to do next, do nothing until you positively do. The universe will help you find the answer you need, but first you must fully understand the problem.

365

❖❖❖

I must be open and honest with the thoughts I think and the words I speak.

(I am I) I am at the heart of the consciousness of man. His thoughts link directly to me. When man lives a life of illusion and dishonesty he becomes slightly disjointed. He looses the strength of his link with me. When his thoughts reflect his inner truth and actions, he is in tune with me. He is in tune with life itself. (I am I)

Just for today, keep nothing hidden and speak your truth, but do it with kindness and love. Do not let your thoughts run riot in your head, but instead bring them back to now. The universe needs the input that is yours, so speak your mind in the matter that concerns you the most.

366

❖❖❖

I must be true to my inner self.

Man has much work to do to balance his character and clear his clutter, but once this has been correctly achieved his internal self will be a pool of wealth and support.

The life of man contains many lessons, but he also collects a lot of rubbish, and it is this that needs to be cleared. Not just physically, but mentally.

Your higher self will always know what is best for you, but often you think you do so yourself. When you make your own choices and are still not happy, you have not heard a word that it said.

Just for today, do not rush forward in impulse or speed; instead just step back and reassess. There are many ways to achieve the goal you desire, but only one will be true and correct. Send your thoughts out to the God, to Source and allow higher truth to come in.

367

❖ ❖ ❖

I must be vigilant everyday to choose the right and discard the wrong...

Positive and negative influences exist everywhere constantly.

(I am I) Man is the instigator of his own life. He alone chooses it. He creates his experiences, but not his influences. These exist everywhere as part of the life he can choose from. What he does and what he chooses is up to him entirely. He is here to experience life and happiness. (I am I)

Not all choices are for the better. Many will lead him astray and bring him sorrow. This is the influence of free will and outside pressure. To know who he is, he must also know clearly the person he is not. From the ashes of disaster roses bloom best. No man can ever be immune from the negative, but he can choose to move away from it as soon as he realizes or desires.

Just for today, be aware of the influences that could also lead you astray. Look for those that are better. You create your reality every minute of everyday. Learn to make the choice that is for the highest good. Always.

368

❖ ❖ ❖

I must be wise to the trickery of my own thoughts.

The thoughts of man do not always stick to the truth. They will lead him down the tricky path of lies and illusion just as easily as the blink of his eye. It is up to him to realize the difference.

The thoughts of man do not rule his life. He does this for himself. When he is not careful his state of mind can lead him right down the garden path. He will come to completely the wrong conclusion, simply because he has not allowed himself to know or believe the actual truth.

There are only two modes of thought in existence – love and fear. All that stems after is but a subdivision of these categories. To be in the love is to have an open, balanced and positively receptive mind to the truth of the situation, whether you want to hear it or not. To be in the fear is everything else – jealousy, doubt, worry, mistrust, disbelief etc. Illusion is built upon illusion until only illusion is left.

Just for today, be aware of the patterns of your thoughts. Are you building a picture of fear and illusion? Do you think you know the outcome before it has even begun? Send all your thoughts up to God, to Source, that they can be removed from your mind. Allow each moment to unfold as it must, without excess thought in any one direction. Let your mind be at peace and let the love come in. The highest outcome will be given to you.

369

❖ ❖ ❖

I must be true to my better side.

Man knows the difference between right and wrong, even when his brothers think not.

Man has an inbuilt knowing system. He can walk into a situation and instantly have a feel for it. He knows where he fits and where he does not. He is plugged into the truth of the world. Yet often he ignores his knowing. He continues forward even when he realizes he should not. He chooses to push past his intuitive guidance.

Just for today, follow your inner guidance. You are more in tune with life than you think. Use the knowledge you have gained to date and let your mind be open to your higher truth.

370

❖ ❖ ❖

I must trust that I will receive all that I need if I stay true to the good.

You are a being of love and light.

(I am I) The work you have achieved in clearing your space can never be for nothing. You are joining back as one with the one light. You are tuning yourself back into the frequency of the Earth. You are coming home to where you have always belonged. (I am I)

No one but you can know how far you have come. Each man must take his own journey, but all will ultimately lead to the same goal – to God.

When you live each day to its highest good you will always be looked after. You walk in tune with life. You are a worker of light. You move it and take it wherever you go. It is who and what you are. You need do no more than be your true self. All other things will follow and flow.

Just for today, know that when you work and live with the highest good, that all your needs will be met. The centre of the universe begins with you. You put the creative energy to use. All that you are was born from your mind.

(I am I) All of the Earth stemmed from mine. (I am I)

371

❖❖❖

I must recognize when I take a wrong choice and correct it immediately.

When you take the wrong route you can know it instantly.

You are in tune with your energy. You are in tune with life. You know the difference between good and wrong vibrations.

Life will try to lead you in many directions you have no further need to go. You have grown beyond them. There is nothing for you in the place of the past. Your time is now. You create your reality now. You can see through illusions. You know what matters. You know where you have been, what you have let go, and you know the truths that really count.

Just for today, do not be afraid to say no. You can take a U-turn whenever you choose. You have learnt that you can choose, and to you that is worth a lot. Be attentive to the life that you create. Be true to the being that is you.

372

❖❖❖

I must release myself from the dismissive behaviour of others.

The way that others see you is not always the way they should.

Before you knew your true self it was easy to judge yourself by the views and opinions of others.

(I am I) You are the judge and the jury of yourself. You are in essence the light of the world. You had only to know your true worth. You had only to know you are loved. The being that is you has let the armour fall, and in doing so it has let love in too. (I am I)

Just for today, let others have their opinion. It cannot touch nor harm you anymore. You know the truth. They as yet might not. Send all their words up to the God mind and ask that peace be yours instead. All people will learn the truth one day, but you are privy to it now.

373

❖ ❖ ❖

I am not my mistakes.

Life cannot stand still, but nor can it charge forever onward.

Growth must come in fits and starts. First the initial spurt of pure, creative energy. You know exactly what you must do and the direction in which you must travel, but when you get there too soon there is nothing for you to do. You have got there too soon. For your arrival to bear fruit you must allow everyone else in life to get their connections in order. You are a single piece in a picture, rarely the whole picture itself.

The opposite is true when you travel too slowly. You miss the connections that were put into place to meet you. You were late and they have moved on. But when the timing is perfect, all connections will follow on as they should. Your input will have claimed the place that was destined for you.

Just for today, look for the mistakes that happen around you. Somebody's timing is probably out of sync. When an avenue pans out to nothing, then it was not destined to be taken quite just yet. It may not even have been for you in the first place. When mistakes keep occurring, then something else needs to be addressed. Find out what the problem is and correct it before you move on to the next place.

374

❖❖❖

I am happiness and light.

(I am I) The light will always follow the dark as day will always follow night. Happiness is always there to be recognized, even in the darkest of hours. Man must only recognize its form and be prepared to let it come in. (I am I)

The light of the world shone forth, even after the darkest of hours became fact.

Man has the gift of choice. Man is the master of his reality. Many different worlds exist, because man is the owner of mind, and mind will roam wherever it is able. Man must be in charge of mind so that he can keep it channelled and in order. Man can never be immune from the things that life will throw into his path. He cannot be, because that would render him robotic and without feeling, but he does control his reaction and interaction. He can choose whether he will buckle and break under the weight or whether he will help himself rise above it as soon as he feels that he can.

The universe will always bring light into places of darkness and despair. No discrimination is given. Fear and negative thought, sadness and heartache are everywhere, visiting everyone, everyday, but once it is over it is over, until it begins again. Between the highs and lows that are part and parcel of life, learn to find the reasons. Learn to recognize the part you play in what has been placed in your vision. The choices you make from this moment on will determine the rest of your time.

(I am I) This is the life you will live. Little by little, step by step.

I will help you go forward. I will be right by your side. (I am I)

Just for today, look for the hand that is with you. When you are down, find the up. When you are alone, find the company. When you have troubles, recycle them to spirit and wait for the solution to come.

(I am I) I cannot do the legwork, but I can help to put things into perspective and place. (I am I)

Don't do anything until suddenly you know what to do, but make sure it takes the form of goodness and love.

(I am I) It is only in this place that you can find me. I am only goodness, truth, light and love. I am the light that surrounds you. I am in all that is. (I am I)

375

❖❖❖

I am connected to God.

(I am I) The world is a constantly revolving, growing mechanism, not only in the sphere of the planet itself, but on the surface where man interacts with man and also with nature. (I am I)

Your contribution to the planet is the life you live and the being that you are. Do you help or use the resources you have without thought? Are you loving and giving, in balance and in truth with life, or are you always taking advantage of the situations you encounter? Do you live within your means, or do you borrow heavily right into the future? Are you happy and focused, or do you bemoan each day as you look at your lot? Do you give laughter and uplift to others, or do you look for others to uplift you?

Just for today, take a watchful view of the person you are and your connection to life. The human race can never be perfect, but you must be responsible for the life that you own. When the cap fits you don't have to keep it on, you can choose to change it for a more appropriate environmentally friendly one. Ask with your thoughts that you find the tools that will help you move forward for your highest good.

376

❖❖❖

I trust in the power that is mine.

The power of thought is responsible for the entire world that we see. Everything was once a thought in the mind of an ordinary person. Every thought is linked to the world of possibility and it is by careful choice and action that many are brought to life and matter.

The people who today are known as extraordinary or masters were first and foremost ordinary individuals – the likes of you and I. They did ordinary things that with practice amounted to more. The gifted and talented excel in their individual fields, but many are just ordinary people who when focused can connect to extraordinary levels. Many connect entirely with the world of spirit in their most creative inspirational moments. Many work with spirit co-workers who express their talents through the physical vessel of their choice and nearest likeness. This book was written in this way. The author is just the vessel that the world of spirit is using to portray some higher truths needed at this time in Earth's history of evolution.

Just for today, look for the extraordinary interventions in your own life. When you find yourself wondering what something would be like, try it. Do it. Send your thoughts upstairs and ask for the inspiration and courage you need. Not all exploits will lead to mastery, but unless you try, how can you know?

377

❖❖❖

My connection to God remains pure and true.

Man is a vessel for energy to pulse through. The thoughts and deeds that he lives by determine the pureness of energy he produces.

(I am I) I am the light. Man is potentially shades of that light. How brightly he shines will be up to him. No man can be perfect, because he lives in this physical world wrought with distraction and decay, but man is capable of stepping out and beyond the confines of his surroundings. He can choose to make the best of the lot that he owns. (I am I)

Man can do as he pleases and all things are acceptable, providing they remain in full balance with the whole of the rest of his life.

(I am I) The World is me and I am the World. All that occurs I

know about. How could I not when the body that gives you life is mine? I ask that you live life to the full, but to the degradation of no man and no thing. All that you are, you are so by choice, until the time that you choose it no more. How could I condemn you for experiencing all that now is? I ask only that you remember you account for your actions. You have responsibility for yourself and for the role you then have on others. This life is for you to live and to choose, and when you find your choices were not as you hoped, you have the choice once again to move on. How can you become your best when you have no experience to measure against? When the life that you choose does more harm than good, it is time for you to move on. (I am I)

Just for today, keep your thoughts focused on your highest intention. Help others who are stuck to do the same. At the end of the day when you don't enjoy life, you short change nobody but own yourself. Sit down, take a break and find the centre of your being. Close your eyes, take some deep breaths until you know exactly where you are. The peace of the Earth will connect at these times and bring the connection that is yours back to truth. Take a moment or two to sit with your space and go forward to the light that is you.

378

❖❖❖

I will be all that I am.

A seed is nondescript, but it knows how it must be.

Man is born of man, but his body does not limit him. He is not limited by his parentage. He is not limited by his surroundings, yet he limits himself by his mind.

Man is not controlled by mind; instead he has charge over it.

Man thinks he is tied up by life, but he ties himself up in his knots.

Man believes he is his body – his shell. He believes his body is his all, yet it is not.

Man has no limits other than those he places upon himself.

Just for today, know that all you are destined to be, you will be. You have the whole of your life to do it. You have the tools of the Earth in your hand. You have the use of the God mind, of Source, at all time. You are connected to the all that is. You are everything you should be – now. The rest will come when it will.

379
❖❖❖

I have life now.

Now is the only time frame that exists, as we know it. Now is where life turns energy into matter.

All that man thinks - forms matter. All that he does - makes matter solid. Man has the power of creation. He creates with everyday that is.

Man has control of all life. He can recycle the negative and bring forth the positive to take its place. The choice is always his. He has only to realize and remain focused and aware.

The life you have left must be used to the full. Take charge of the gift that it is.

Just for today, recognize the importance of you. You hold a unique space on this Earth. You are the living link in the line of your heritage. Be proud of the being that you are. You have the gift of time now.

(I Am I)

Life is too short to let it slip through the fingers.

Man must harness his life.

This he must learn to do.

This he must practice.

(I Am I)

Energy

❖❖❖

Energy is the life force of this living planet. It is both the essence of man and of spirit. Energy must flow freely in every direction. It takes on the form of its source, it becomes matter as it slows down in frequency, it follows the flow of speech, of thought and of action, it exists in the form of all seen and unseen, all space and all matter surrounding man. Man is the prime source of its transference.

Energy is Energy – it's Intelligent.

Energy is capable of becoming matter when its natural flow and pattern is dense enough. With no boundaries and rules to follow Energy becomes whatever it's allowed... Energy must flow, or it becomes stagnant and stale and loses its vitality and life. Energy that has no life - is dead, it becomes a blockage. It must remain in constant flux to stay alive. Energy is life. Energy itself is Everlasting.

Energy is the life that flows through man and all things.

Energy is the intelligence that is every man/woman/child, every animal, every plant and form of life. Being both positive and negative, Energy becomes the true life that gives life to life. It becomes the best and the worst in us all - both the block and the blockage disperser, it becomes the all that is left when all else has been and gone. Energy can break up the world, but Energy also is that which can save it.

Energy is the divine gift that brings life and love to man.

Energy birthed the World – it is the World, it is but the collective thoughts and dreams of the planet itself. Energy became this living planet. With no beginning there is also no end. Energy can transcend time and space because it knows nothing about time. It has no limitation, no ties, no form of its own until it is directed to become.

Energy is the blind fury of the weather, it is the water that is the sea, the density of rock and the weightlessness of cloud.

Energy is the form of all we see. It is the thought of the future, the weight of the past, the creative living force of here and now. It is thoughts flowing through our head, the birth of each new life and the dawn of every day that we awake. It follows our wants and dreams, but it is also the main cause of our destruction.

Energy has been waging a battle since the time the World began. It must sustain itself in order to exist - it needs positive thoughts and the love of man to help it. It must rely on man - to begin to understand its meaning, and to understand its role within his life, as well as in the world he sees around him.

Energy is the planet itself.

Paul

Conclusion

❖❖❖

From this point forward, if we all used the time we have left upon Earth to its highest possible good and advantage, by the time we returned home, back to the spirit world, we'd be amazed at what we've put into action – just because we bothered to wake up, because we turned ourselves around and because we tried to help life make a difference.

Life needs each one of us to wake up to its truth just as soon as we possibly can. In times gone past it took a whole life time to build up a home, to raise a family and maintain a career. Today things are different. We live many lives and go through many life changes – within one life. We realise that when we get there – nothing's changed, nothing's different. We're no happier inside than we were before.

It used to be enough that upon our return to the spirit world, when we reviewed life and mistakes we had made, that we would promise next time to do better. But no longer. Time is no longer that friend. Just look at the world you see around you, not just out there, but closer at your family and friends...

Through the growth of technology and the pace we all live at, mistakes are going too deep. We travel miles along a wrong path before we understand or recognise that we should stop. It is up to us all individually – to wake up to now, while we're still physically incarnated on Earth. Only on this physical level can changes and shifts be immediate, selective and permanent.

We have the task of putting things right, of unblocking our own selves where we are stuck and for setting life straight for our children. How can we expect them to sort out what we in our own time could not? And is it fair?

This book was not written to be a bible of life. Its lessons are but reminders and tools to help us all again find our way, to reconnect the divine connection we thought we'd lost. This is a strong three way link between yourself, your own guardian and God.

We can never disconnect from the planet that gives us life – we only have to realise this as fact. The truest things that matter have always been within our own reach.

We are our own masters. We have nothing to prove and no one to prove anything to, except ourselves. When our life goes astray, we are responsible for the wake we leave behind. We are responsible for our interaction within life and with other people, for the times we accidentally or deliberately send things astray. The mark we place on the life that we've spent is ours to be proud to own up to. We have Earth's power at our feet, in all we say and do, and nothing can be mightier than that.

We have the trust of God. If we have any trust at all in the life that is ours – we must trust in the life that is God. Together we can change today – to build a better future.

Further Reading

❖ ❖ ❖

The following list is merely a sample of literature available in the mind, body and spirit or self-help section of your local bookshop.

To connect with your inner self and your own personal guides or angels, simply still your mind for a few minutes and browse through the following list; see which titles you connect with and trust your own inner guidance.

You will be guided one step at a time, along a path that is right for you. When you browse through your bookshop or library, notice the titles that jump out and grab your attention. These are the books most likely to take you forward at this point in your journey.

Never read a book from back to front, always from front to back. Many can be read from beginning to end fairly quickly, but others will be better chapter by chapter, to give the information time to sink in. Because you are on a journey, you will likely experience in your life the things you have read. This is good. It is part of the experience and the same path of learning.

Some books will feel flat in the middle, but don't worry and don't be tempted to skip over these sections. They are flat because at this particular time the information might not relate to your needs. Your mind will simply place it in store until it does.

Other books will be hard going because they are not right for you in your now. Put them down and go back to them at a later date if you wish.

This mode of reading information will help you outgrow outdated boundaries and beliefs that may have lingered with you since your childhood. It is a process that will take you forward from the place you are stuck to where you can operate more efficiently. It will open you up to the flow of life that is waiting to help. It will connect you once more to your guides.

Good Luck!

Stephanie J. King

Juan Arias, *Confessions of a Pilgrim*: Paulo Coelho, HarperCollins, 2001

Richard Bach, *Jonathan Livingston Seagull*, Macmillan, 1970

Richard Bach, *Illusions*, Bantam Doubleday Dell, 1977

Richard Bach, *The Bridge Across Forever*, William Morrow & Co., 1984

Richard Bach, *One*, Bantam Books, 1992

DeSersa Esther Black Elk, Pourier Olivia Black Elk, Lori Utecht and Charles Trimble, *Black Elk Lives: Conversations with the Black Elk Family*, University of Nebraska Press, 2000

Wallace Black Elk and William S. Lyon, *Black Elk Speaks Again*, HarperCollins, 1990

Brian Browne Walker, *The I Ching or Book of Changes*, St Martin's Press, 1992

C. Maxwell Cade and Nana Coxhead, *The Awakened Mind*, Delacorte Press, 1978

Jack Canfield and Mark Victor Hansen, *Chicken Soup for the Soul*, Health Communications, 1993

Patricia Carrington, PhD, *Learning to Meditate*, Pace Educational Systems, 1979

Deepak Chopra, *The Path to Love*, Harmony Books, 1997

Anthea Church, *Inner Beauty*, Brahma Kumaris Information Services Publications, 1995

Paulo Coelho, *The Alchemist*, HarperSanFrancisco, 1993

Paulo Coelho, *The Valkyries*, HarperSanFrancisco, 1995

Paulo Coelho, *The Fifth Mountain*, Thorsons, 1998

Paulo Coelho, *The Pilgrimage*, Thorsons, 1999

Diana Cooper, *A Little Light on Angels*, Findhorn Press, 1996

Diana Cooper, *Angel Inspiration*, Hodder Mobius, 2001

A Course in Miracles, The Foundation for Inner Peace, 1977

Janki Dadi, *Wings of Soul*, Brahma Kumaris Information Services Publications, 1998

Lama Surya Das, *Awakening the Buddha Within*, Bantam Doubleday Dell Publishing Group, 1997

Michael Drosnin, *The Bible Code*, Weidenfeld and Nicolson, 1997

J. Arthur Findlay, *The Rock of Truth*, Psychic Press, 1948

Susan Forward, *Toxic Parents*, Bantam Doubleday Dell Publishing Group, 1989

Shakti Gawain, *Living in the Light*, Harcourt Brace Co., 1986

John Gray, *Men are from Mars and Women are from Venus*, HarperBusiness, 1992

John Gray, *Men are from Mars and Women are from Venus – Children are from Heaven*, Vermilion, 1999

Susi Hayman, *The Relate Guide to Second Families*, Vermilion, 1997

Susan Hayward, *A Guide for the Advanced Soul*, Little, Brown & Co., 1989

James Hillman, *The Soul's Code*, Random House, 1996

Naomi Levy, *To Begin Again*, Random House, 1998

Denise Linn, *Signposts*, Rider, 1996

Sarah Litvinoff, *The Relate Guide to Starting Again*, Vermilion, 1993

Susan Chernak McElroy, *Animals as Teachers and Healers*, Thorndike, 1997

Lynne McTaggart, *The Field*, HarperCollins, 2001

Gustavus Hindman Miller, *A Dictionary of Dreams*, Gallery Books, 1991

Dr H.C. Moolenburgh, *Meetings with Angels*, C.W. Daniel, 1992

John G. Neihardt, *Black Elk Speaks*, University of Nebraska Press, 1992

M. Scott Peck, *The Road Less Traveled*, Hutchinson, 1983

M. Scott Peck, *The Road Less Traveled and Beyond*, Rider, 1997

Edwin Raphael, *The Complete Book of Dreams*, Foulsham, 1992

James Redfield, *The Celestine Prophecy: An Adventure*, Warner Books 1994

James Redfield, *The Tenth Insight*, Warner Books 1996

James Redfield and Carol Adrienne, *The Celestine Prophecy: An Experiential Guide*, Bantam Books, 1995

James Redfield and Carol Adrienne, *The Tenth Insight: An Experiential Guide (for advanced students)*, Time Warner, 1996

John Ruskin, *Emotional Clearing*, R. Wyler & Co., 1993

Betty Shine, *A Mind of Your Own*, HarperCollins, 1998

Robin Skynner and John Cleese, *Families and How to Survive Them*, Methuen, 1983

Stephen Turoff, *Seven Steps to Eternity*, Elmore-Chard, 1989

Iyania Vanzant, *In the Meantime*, Simon & Schuster, 1998

Iyania Vanzant, *One Day My Soul Just Opened Up*, Pocket Books, 1998

Iyania Vanzant, *Yesterday I Cried*, Simon & Schuster, 1999

Neale Donald Walsch, *Conversations with God*, Book 1, G.P. Putnam's Sons, 1996; Book 2, Hampton Roads, 1997; Book 3, Hampton Roads, 1998

Ambika Wauters, *Ambika's Guide to Healing and Wholeness*, Piatkus Books, 1995

Richard Webster, *Spirit Guides and Angel Guardians*, Llewellyn, 1998

Linda Williamson, *Finding the Spirit Within*, Rider, 2000

Dr Brian Weiss, *Messages from the Masters*, Warner Books, 2000

Also by Stephanie J. King

❖ ❖ ❖

And So It Begins...

This is the first book written in a series destined to rebuild the hopes and happiness of Man, who has thought himself unworthy and abandoned for far too long. Man is connected to the true source of life, to the source of the planet itself. He has never been anything other.

Man was born to live the life that is now his. This is his heritage, not his punishment. Man was meant to be happy, living his choices, not down trodden and depressed. *And So It Begins...* mirrors aspects of character that rarely get considered. It helps unburden clutter, blindly passed down through generations. The time that Man has left is the key to his future, and his future begins here and now. This is his legacy.

To view further details on Stephanie J. King, visit:
www.channelledbyspirit.com

A Closing Note from the Author

❖❖❖

This book was given to help you move forward and you will probably use it on and off throughout your life... If you have enjoyed it, then please continue to use it as often as you can, but pass its title and details on to someone new, friend or family, as a tool to aid them the same way.

Remember Spirit needs us just as much as we need them, and that linking Heaven and Earth is a two-way street. By pulling together correctly in the same direction, we can successfully bring peace, love and light back to Earth...

Thank you for being open to the possibility that there is indeed more to life than the struggles we presently know...

Stephanie J. King

NOTES

NOTES

LIFE IS CALLING...

CPSIA information can be obtained
at www.ICGtesting.com
Printed in the USA
LVHW081405090620
657726LV00002B/213